The Courage to Live

The Courage to Live

A Biography of Suzanne de Diétrich

Hans-Ruedi Weber

WCC Publications, Geneva

A fully annotated, enlarged French edition with bibliography
appears as *La passion de vivre: Suzanne de Diétrich*,
Les Bergers et Mages/Oberlin, Paris/Strasbourg, 1995.

Copyright © Hans-Ruedi Weber 1995

Cover illustration: "Resurrection" by Adrian Frutiger
Cover design: Rob Lucas

ISBN 2-8254-1156-6

WCC Publications, World Council of Churches,
150 route de Ferney, 1211 Geneva 2, Switzerland

Printed in Switzerland

Contents

Meeting Suzanne

To come to know Suzanne de Diétrich is to take part in almost a century of world history. This small woman shared in the aspirations and the disappointments of everyone she met during her travels and work in five continents. Deeply marked by two world wars, coping with a congenital infirmity, learning, teaching and writing, she became for many a source of inspiration and hope.

Successive Christian student generations called her simply "Suzanne". Not out of any lack of respect. "As the members of royal families and certain great stars are known by their first name because they belong to the whole world, so Suzanne was 'our Suzanne'," wrote her Dutch friend, Willem A. Visser 't Hooft.

Meeting Suzanne was often a disturbing experience. Jeanne Lebrun, a French teacher, first came into contact with her in 1936. For that young seeker Miss de Diétrich was already a legend: descendant of a well-known industrial family from Alsace in north-eastern France, one of the first women to study engineering, a world student leader just back from an adventurous journey through South America. In Argentina — so it was said — she had chided the pilot because he had hesitated to take off in bad weather to fly over the Andes to Chile. "I do not remember what Suzanne said to me," recalls Lebrun, "but the meeting itself is vivid in my memory — Suzanne with a subtle smile on her lips, a smile expressing tenderness and humour, Suzanne with a withdrawn look in her eyes, remote, as if she were looking into her inner self. I knew I was accepted and supported. Never before had I come across such a quality of listening."

Working with Suzanne in the French Student Christian Movement, Jeanne Lebrun got to know her better: "I came to know the Suzanne who judged. Sometimes she would make very brief remarks, which at the time were hard to accept but whose truth was subsequently apparent. She plunged us into fire and we emerged scarred but all the better for it."

In writing on Suzanne de Diétrich's work, I have made use of her many books and articles. To come to grips with her personality, I found more revealing some of her unpublished manuscripts, the journal she occasionally kept, and above all the several thousand letters written by her or addressed to her and which have been preserved. I interviewed people who knew her well and worked with her in different parts of the world, and many of them have sent written accounts.

Out of this wealth of material the main traits of Suzanne's character emerge. At first there seem to be many contradictions, but gradually the wholeness and coherence which marked her life's journey begin to stand out.

Suzanne remained fervently French, yet at the same time she became a world citizen. To avoid any doubt about her nationality she changed the spelling and pronunciation of her family name by adding an accent: "de Diétrich" (this accent will be kept here when referring to her personally). As her horizon and circle of friends began to reach to the ends of the earth she was inclined to become impatient with those who complacently remained within the borders of France. Once she wrote from an ocean liner, as it steamed across the Atlantic: "A ship's cabin is definitely becoming my favourite home in this world. It is the most suitable lodging for my state of being a 'traveller and pilgrim on this earth', and it gives me a foretaste of eternity."

Suzanne had a scientific training, she excelled in mathematics, yet she became a biblical theologian: an unusual combination, especially for a woman in the early twentieth century. The clarity and precision of an engineer, the sensitivity of a woman and a biblical sense of awe for the mysteries of creation marked her teaching and writing. No wonder she was impatient with sloppy thinking and mere rhetoric in theological discourse, and with people who wanted to reduce reality to what can be seen, measured, bought and sold. Like Blaise Pascal, the French mathematician who became a theological thinker, she saw the misery and greatness of our human condition. Thinking of herself, people in general, and Christians and theologians in particular, she once remarked: "If I were God I would find humanity extremely tiring."

Though a Protestant of the Reformed tradition, Suzanne was completely open to learning from the traditions and spiritualities of Roman Catholic and Orthodox believers and from honest agnostics. Her Protestant faith had been shaped by the special type of socially committed, prophetic and earthly piety which Jean-Frédéric Oberlin had developed in her native Alsace. Like him she called herself a "reformed Catholic". Once she wrote: "I always live Good Friday in close communion with my Protestant friends and Easter Day in close communion with my Orthodox friends." This openness enabled her to become a pioneer of the growing ecumenical movement, that development in nineteenth- and twentieth-century church history which draws together Christians of all confessional families and all continents for witnessing and serving more faithfully in the "oikoumene", the whole inhabited world.

A militant woman, Suzanne nevertheless avoided polemics and worked for reconciliation. "I want to fight or not to live at all," she wrote as a teenager. She came of a hot-tempered family, was given to sudden outbursts of anger, sometimes over trivial things, and could on such occasions hurt people. More often, however, her anger had to do with the causes for which she fought: peace with justice, intellectual honesty, courage in thought and action. Suzanne had a sense of humour, and she was ready to ask for forgiveness, so people were rarely offended by her fits of anger. She liked to draw opposing parties into a common search for fuller truth and a willingness to learn from one another's partial perceptions of truth. She could not stand self-righteousness and self-complacency. For her, serious biblical interpreters were those who did not take themselves seriously, for they knew their limitations and were aware of the fact that their work was based on the work of many others.

Suzanne was physically handicapped, but she was a great traveller who always wanted to see what lay beyond. With her short arms and stiff legs she had to walk with two sticks. How frustrating to walk so slowly when she wanted to run and dance! How annoying not to be able to bend down and wash her own feet! Character and humour helped, and very few people ever heard Suzanne complain about her infirmity. With obstinate courage and a readiness to take risks she went travelling at a time when there were no provisions for people with physical handicaps: climbing up and down the steps of railway carriages, sitting with her two sticks on the baggage holder of a bicycle while a student pedalled her through the city traffic of Paris or Geneva. Her curiosity made her explore what lies beyond our time. During the last war she wrote: "I often look at the tremendous page of history God is writing, with the expectancy and amazement of a child waiting for the end of the story."

What people remember vividly and cherish with gratitude is Suzanne's great gift of friendship. She was a trusted friend of children whom she fascinated with her travel stories; of young people whose questions she took seriously; of suffering persons in need of material and spiritual help; of colleagues with whom she worked, whom she challenged to competitive games (she hated losing!) and with whom she enjoyed a good meal and good wine. Her hospitality was proverbial.

Once she had just moved into a new flat in Geneva when a student who was staying with her told her about a leprosy patient who was looking for temporary lodging. With her stick Suzanne pointed to the guest-room and said: "Well then, your friend shall be the first guest in our room for friends." But here too there was a contradiction. Suzanne often needed to be alone, away from people. Amidst God's creation, with an uncommon empathy she was then in communion with the sea and the mountains, with birds and animals and particularly with trees.

Despite all the contrasting traits in Suzanne's character, there was a wholeness and single-mindedness which was astonishing in a world and time marked by so much fragmentation. That coherence stemmed from the most fundamental contrast: Suzanne was passionately present both on this earth *and* in a world and time beyond our own. Her life had a prophetic and transcendental quality. She anticipated many of the questions which are urgently discussed today and she pioneered in areas which are only now being dealt with. Through her "double presence", now and in eternity, Suzanne could suddenly fall silent in a conversation or in a group as if she were involved in another dialogue, bringing before God what was being said and planned on earth. Her life with its varied involvements was thus constantly focused on God and the coming kingdom. She also had a way of drawing those she thought about and those she talked to out of this time's confusion into the realm of eternity.

None has expressed this better than Suzanne's Scottish friend and colleague, Robert C. Mackie. With his gift of discerning what is unique in a person he wrote in 1948: "She always had a holy horror of all conventional piety, and this is exactly why she could help so many people in the life of the Spirit. The most unusual and charming side of her personality is perhaps a certain other-worldly quality — not that of a cloister, but of woods and hills." During the second world war Suzanne wrote to Mackie in Canada, telling him how, in Geneva, she felt imprisoned by the closed frontiers and how in a dream she felt "carried back to the Canadian woods, listening to the life of the forest. If I believed in a previous life I would say I must have been a loon." Commenting on that letter Mackie remarked: "Thinking of this strange, unreal bird uttering its cry over the dark waters of a lake, I came to understand Suzanne de Diétrich better — and also the gospel. For Suzanne is a little like a fairy from another world: when grace penetrates and conquers that inner world from which intelligence springs, it appears in its full power. And it is this power of grace which our friend has shown in her writings, in her words, and in the courage of her life."

1
Awakening to Life

"If you were a boy, what would you do?"

Suzanne was fifteen and already an orphan when the question was put to her. Being a de Dietrich, born into a family which owned a large industrial firm, her answer was not surprising: "I would become an engineer." The response she received was less predictable and, for the end of the nineteenth century, quite unexpected: "Well, why not?" [1]

A small teenager with a congenital infirmity, was she to become an engineer? Years later she still remembered her initial reaction. Engineering was not what she really wanted to do, "but the main thing is to get out of here".

A dark childhood

The stately mansion where Suzanne was born on 29 January 1891 is situated just outside Niederbronn in northern Alsace, north-east France. It is called the "Moulin", the mill, because in its grounds stands one of the many water mills to be found in the border region of the Vosges. It also has a park with beautiful trees. Why did Suzanne want to get out of this lovely and protective environment?

Until recently little was known about the early years of Suzanne's life. She seldom spoke about her childhood and family. Friends knew that she kept personal papers and letters in old suitcases; some years after her death they were found in the attic of the "Moulin" and their contents were donated to the national library in Strasbourg, to become in 1990 the main collection of the Suzanne de Diétrich Archives. [2] The correspondence covers a long period, 1907 to 1981. In addition, there are a number of documents written by Suzanne, some of her notebooks and diaries, and three fragments of autobiographical notes.

In one of these notes Suzanne wrote about her childhood: "My childhood: a time gone past, a kind of middle ages of the industrial era. It is as though I can still hear the workers walking along the road, at 5.30 in the morning and 6.30 in the evening. Some had to walk eight or ten kilometers to their place of work. The barons de Dietrich reigned over quite an area. My father was responsible for the foundries, my uncle for the large factory in Reichshoffen."[3] "I was a late-comer and probably little welcome." Suzanne was the youngest of seven children, all girls. Two of the sisters had died at an early age. It was a difficult delivery, and her mother was ill for the rest of her life. Like her father and three of her older sisters, Suzanne had genetic deformations, short arms and legs. She was a lonely child: "I can't remember any of my sisters ever playing with me. During my early childhood I saw no other children, I just dreamed."

In the beginning she enjoyed dreaming. The little girl cheerfully made the rounds of the park on her bicycle and told herself stories. The rounds brought her back again and again to two large sequoias. She watched them grow taller and taller, and these Californian giants became very special trees for her.

Soon, however, the dreaming was no longer happy. She felt lonely and friendless. "My first memory was the bony face of my wet-nurse, with her braid of brown hair. I shed many tears the day Käthe left me, by the small garden door. 'She will have a husband and her own little girl,' they told me. I had no idea what 'a husband' meant. A little girl? Wasn't I enough for her?... The nannies succeeded one another. As soon as I could write I composed great declarations of love to them: 'My dear Fanny who will never leave me...'"

It is significant that Suzanne's first recorded memory is not of parents or sisters, but of her wet-nurse. Family life in the "Moulin" was not a happy one. There were too many illnesses, tensions and deaths. When at eight little Suzanne saw a village marriage she pointed to the newly-weds and exclaimed: "Poor things! They don't know what they are doing."

The parents

Suzanne's mother, the Baroness Anne von Türcke (1848-1900), came from a noble family from the Thüringer forests of Germany, whose origins can be traced back to sixteenth-century Karinthia in southern Austria. One of her ancestors became the adviser to the duke of Sachsen-Meiningen, and his descendants occupied various positions in that small German dukedom. Among them was Georg Ludwig von Türcke (1814-88), Suzanne's maternal grandfather, who was also a cousin of Suzanne's father. The nobility of Alsace, especially the de Berckheims and the de Dietrichs, had several marriage connections with the noble families of

Sachsen-Meiningen, particularly with the von Steins, the von der Tanns and the von Türckes.

The small dukedom of Sachsen-Meiningen had its court theatre, concerts and literary activities. Ludwig Brechstein, who collected German fairy tales, had worked there; the composers Richard Strauss and Max Reger were directors of the court orchestra. In the letters Suzanne wrote during her many visits to Meiningen there was no mention of that cultural life. She only wrote about "the forests and the fields of wheat", and at times commented on the anti-French remarks made by the von Türckes, particularly Baron Ludwig, one of her godfathers.

Suzanne remembered her mother sitting in a large armchair, a woman of great distinction, very pale and with clear blue eyes. As a little girl she wanted to climb on her mother's lap, but one of her sisters would invariably say: "Don't tire mama." She particularly remembered an evening in May 1900 when, now nine years old, she ran excitedly to her mother's room to tell her that she had given a first French lesson to the gardener's boy. "My mother told me softly: 'You will tell me this tomorrow, I am tired.' Next morning at six thirty I heard people weeping. My father came to my room and said: 'Your mother is in heaven.'"

Suzanne's father, Baron Charles de Dietrich (1841-1906), was a strange person. People respected him because he belonged to the noble family that ruled over the countryside. They also feared him because of his fiery temperament. His great passion was hunting. Sometimes he took young Suzanne with him on his wild hunting expeditions in the woods. "When we brought back a bleeding roe with its large, sorrowful eyes which seemed full of reproach, I was happy for my father but sorry for the poor animal. Two of my sisters also had a passion for hunting. As for myself, the look of the roebucks has always haunted me."

When Baron Charles died on a Saturday morning in 1906, after weeks of illness, the five daughters weeping and crying by his bedside, the factory bells went on ringing for a full hour. The funeral was a spectacular event. Three years later Suzanne wrote: "After the death of papa everybody wept for him, yet I felt calm, in communion with him, nearer to him than when he was alive."

The Alsatian background

To understand the atmosphere in Suzanne's family it is important to remember the turbulent history and political situation of Alsace. Ever since the Celts and the Germanic tribes populated the fertile plain between the Rhine and the mountain range of the Vosges, the region had been a zone of contention. French and German politics, culture and language interpenetrated and confronted each other. By the end of the Thirty Years War (1618-48) most of Alsace had been conquered by the French armies. When in 1681 the city of Strasbourg also capitulated and submitted to King Louis XIV, Alsace became part of France. It developed culturally and economically. Many welcomed the French Revolution and, after the years of terror, even more the conquests of Napoleon whose armies included a large number of Alsatian volunteers with over sixty generals from the region. After Napoleon's defeat the Congress of Vienna in 1815 decreed that Alsace should remain part of France. The large majority of the population consisted of farmers and factory workers speaking Alsatian, a German dialect. The nobility spoke French and looked upon Paris as their political and cultural centre.

The situation changed when in 1870 Napoleon III declared war on the Prussians. That year his armies suffered a shattering defeat near the de Dietrich factories of Reichshoffen. The treaty of Frankfurt in 1871 incorporated part of Lorraine and the whole of Alsace into the Prussian empire as a "Reichsland". Many among the Alsatian higher classes emigrated to "the interior", as they called metropolitan France. They were able to keep their estates, and used to spend their vacations in Alsace. The de Dietrich family decided to stay back.

Suzanne was thus a German citizen at birth. At the "Moulin" wet-nurses, maids, gardeners and coachmen came from the region and spoke Alsatian, but the de Dietrich family members spoke French. Suzanne's German mother was no friend of the Prussians and she spoke a better French than most of her Alsatian sisters-in-law. Nevertheless, the situation in the German-ruled Alsace after the French defeat in 1870 must have added to the tension in Suzanne's home.

The atmosphere became even more depressing because of a series of deaths: Suzanne's mother, then an uncle, and later her father. After each death the family wore black for three years. No wonder Suzanne had a *mémoire noire*, a black memory of her childhood.

Mademoiselle Boillot

The fact that Louise Boillot, Suzanne's private tutor, always wore a long black cape must have reinforced this. The de Dietrich daughters nicknamed her the "abbé".

Boillot was tutor, governess, older companion and foster-mother to Suzanne, and played a decisive role in Suzanne's growth into maturity. Little is known about her. She came from a humble working-class family and had no teacher's diploma, but before coming to Niederbronn she had gained experience as a private tutor in Paris. An intelligent and strong-minded person, she began by correcting the strong Alsatian accent in Suzanne's French and taught her to write correctly the language of La Fontaine and Descartes. Together with her pupil she read and critically discussed a wide range of classical and modern authors. She also helped the dreamy child to look realistically at the world around her. When she was eighty Suzanne recalled that Boillot had opened her eyes to the social injustices of the time and the misery of the poor. Up to 1914 most of Suzanne's letters contained references to "Mlle B" who for fifteen years shared her joys and sorrows, work days and vacations. "She loved me as if I had been her own child, with an exclusive and slightly tyrannical attachment of which perhaps only a real mother can free herself."

With Boillot Suzanne experienced in her "black" childhood moments of joy and beauty. In early 1900 they spent two months in Munich for therapy. The nine-year old girl remembered not only the pain of the treatment but also the beautiful things she saw. Munich was for her — before she came to know Paris — "*the* great city". During the summer of the same year the de Dietrich daughters were sent, after the death of their mother, to Parané, a seaside resort on the north coast of Brittany. The children played "burial" on the shore and one day the horrified Mademoiselle Boillot found her little protégée three-quarters buried in the sand.

During her childhood and youth Suzanne spent many summer vacations in such seaside resorts or in the Swiss Alps for cures, always with Boillot. She never tired of admiring the sea, the glaciers and mountain peaks and the forests in Thüringen and in her native Alsace. All her life creation remained a source of inspiration to her.

The five sisters

The five daughters of Charles and Anne de Dietrich had quite different destinies. Like Suzanne, all of them wanted to "get out of here". All did in fact leave Alsace, and none except Suzanne is buried there. Their ways took different directions. [4]

Marie, the oldest, born in 1872, returned to the same country and noble family from which her mother had come: in 1906 she was married to Hugo August von Türcke of Meiningen. This displeased Suzanne who was at that time almost chauvinistically French. When she got news of the birth of Marie's first child, she was deeply unhappy. Later, however, she rejoiced with her sister in the arrival of "a small German boy", and in the following years often went to visit Marie and her family in Meiningen. *Marguerite*, the second daughter, was born in 1874. She never married; France was her passion. It was probably Marguerite who taught Suzanne to read. After the early death of their parents she moved with her younger sisters into a house at Wolfershoffen near Reichshoffen which she and Suzanne had inherited. It had served as a paper mill and was therefore called the "Papéterie" (stationers). Here Marguerite tended her garden and tried to keep the orphaned sisters together. This house became Suzanne's home during vacations. From 1912 onwards Marguerite spent a good deal of her time in Canada, and later settled in British Columbia.

The third daughter, *Amélie*, born in 1875, had artistic gifts. After the death of her mother she went to Austria for lessons in painting. Then farming became an even greater passion. She sold her assets in the de Dietrich factories and bought land in Virginia, USA. A British gentleman farmer, Thomas Trew, the brother of a girl she had met in Austria, joined her, and later they were married. In 1912 they emigrated to Western Canada. It was with Amélie and her children and grandchildren that Suzanne maintained the closest contact. On almost all her later teaching tours to North America she went to British Columbia to visit the Trew family.

Adèle, the fourth daughter, was born in 1880, the only one among the five sisters with no physical disability. In 1907 she left home with a man who was already married, Jacques Pfalzgraf, a coachman employed by the de Dietrichs. They went to the United States where they bought, with Adèle's money, a farm in Fairfax, Virginia. The head of the de Dietrich family ordered all links with her to be cut, and forbade her sisters to write to or visit Adèle. Pfalzgraf was a good husband and a capable farmer, but with a growing number of children they had a difficult time. Adèle felt bitter and lonely, and wrote pathetic letters to her sisters, but at first she received no answers. As soon as Suzanne reached the age of maturity she started writing to her. Later, she helped the family financially and visited them in the United States.

Kings of iron

The walls of the various de Dietrich mansions in and around Niederbronn were adorned not only with antlers and paintings of hunting scenes, but also with the portraits of Suzanne's ancestors. As a child she felt intimidated by them. Merchants and bankers, politicians and industrialists, they had played a prominent role in Alsatian history.[5]

The line started with Demange Didier, the descendant of a rich Protestant merchant family from Lorraine. Fearing the persecution of Protestants by the Catholic duke of Lorraine, he came in 1561 as a twelve-year old youth to Protestant Strasbourg, at that time a free city within the German empire. He worked with the business firm of the de Turckheims and changed his name to Dominicus (Sonntag) Dietrich. His son, Jean Dietrich, started his own business. Through his marriage and able management of his business he soon gained a leading position in Strasbourg.

The industrial venture of the family started in 1684 when Jean Dietrich II bought the ironworks of the Jaegerthal valley near Niederbronn. His grandson Jean III (1719-95) became the first great head of the enterprise. King Louis made him a peer in 1761, and later the German Emperor Franz I of Habsburg conferred on him the title "baron of the holy Roman empire". In pre-revolutionary France only nobility could own land. Baron Jean III now bought large tracts of land and forests, notably the seigneuries of Ober- and Niederbronn and of Reichshoffen. With the immense resources of forests and the increasing number of foundries the de Dietrich enterprise produced iron for the needs of half Alsace and beyond, while in their factories various iron products for household, industry and army were manufactured. In 1771 Baron Jean III, the "king of iron", acquired the county of Ban de la Roche in the Bruche valley of the Vosges which included the ironworks of Rothau. There the de Dietrich lineage met with Jean-Frédéric Oberlin, the pastor and social reformer of Ban de la Roche who inspired a group of men whom Suzanne later acknowledged as her spiritual ancestors. In his will Baron Jean III wrote proudly: "I acquired my fortune without reproach and made thousands of poor people happy." The radical wing of the French Revolution did not think so; they imprisoned him and his family.

His son, Philippe Frédéric de Dietrich (1748-93), was a well-known mineralogist and a highly-cultured representative of the Age of Enlightenment. His many scientific and political functions left him little time for the family busines. As the old regime in France began to crumble he got involved with the hopes and turmoils of the French Revolution. He became the first constitutionally elected mayor of Strasbourg, and was twice re-elected. Most French history books recall that it was in the salon of this mayor that on 26 April 1792 Rouget de l'Isle first sang his "war song for the army of the Rhine" (later called the "Marseillaise" because revolutionaries from Marseilles sang it when they invaded the Tuileries in Paris and overthrew the royal power). In fact it was not the composer de l'Isle but Suzanne's ancestor, Baron Philippe Frédéric, who first sang this song.

Soon after the celebration came the terror. The radical party of the Jacobins denounced the mayor. His father, wife and children were imprisoned and all the goods of the de Dietrich family confiscated. Following considerable intrigue, Baron Philippe Frédéric was condemned to death, and went to the guillotine in Paris during the final days of 1793. Suzanne did not talk much about these events, but it is significant that when in 1914 she bought reproductions of her "saints", Rouget de l'Isle was one of them.

In the chaos left by the Revolution it looked as if the kings of iron had no future. Philippe Frédéric's son, Fritz de Dietrich (1773-1806), embarked on a military career and was highly regarded in the circles of Napoleon Bonaparte, but ill-health and the sad state of the family business forced him to abandon this career. Through indemnities received for losses during the Revolution and by selling property, including the ironworks of Rothau, he just managed to avoid bankruptcy. But then he died, leaving a 29-year-old widow and four young children.

His wife, however, proved herself to be a strong and innovative business woman. Amélie-Louise de Dietrich-de Berckheim (1776-1855), Suzanne's great-grandmother, created the "Widow de Dietrich and Sons" company and saw to it that her two sons, Albert and Eugène, completed industrial studies. Her son-in-law, Baron Guillaume de Turckheim, and later also her two sons were associated with the management of the firm. This led to restructuring, and resources were found to buy up competing foundries in the region. Amélie is remembered not only for her entre-preneurial abilities; she was one of the four "Demoiselles de Berckheim", known in Alsatian literature for their correspondence which gives a vivid picture of how daughters of a noble family experienced daily life and the historic events before and during the French Revolution, the Napoleonic wars and the subsequent period of the restoration. The de Berckheim sisters occasionally invited Oberlin to come and give them lessons. Not only Suzanne herself but her great-grandmother as well was thus influ-enced by Oberlin's faith and vision. But unlike her great-grandmother and other ancestors, she never had to guide a large industrial enterprise through difficult times. But she did continue to write letters in the "Demoiselles de Berckheim" tradition.

A stained-glass Christ

As a twelve-year old girl, Suzanne occasionally had to preside over family worship at the "Moulin". The worship was held each morning and conducted in German because of the ten servants who also attended it.

Usually Baron Charles read a one-page meditation and Suzanne's task was to recite the Lord's prayer. When her father and her oldest sister were absent, as was often the case, the other sisters passed on to her the task of conducting the worship.

However, these duties and the obligatory attendance at the Lutheran Sunday morning service in the German language were not conducive to awakening any religious fervour in the dreamy girl. The de Dietrich family had a pew in the choir of the church facing the pulpit, and Suzanne recalled: "I understood nothing of the sermons and got very bored. I wanted to uncross my hands when the pastor prayed for the Prussian emperor Wilhelm in order to dissociate myself from the prayer, but I only managed to do so by the time he was praying for the empress."[6]

But in the church there was a stained-glass window representing Christ, and it was this, and not the pastor's sermons, which began to speak to Suzanne: "He looked straight at me. Gradually an intimacy grew between the Christ of this window and myself. After the death of my mother I went to church more readily because of this stained-glass window and the blessing which I felt descended on me. He came to me in this primitive way, through the eyes and not through the ears."

NOTES

[1] SdD; this and following quotation from a five-page manuscript, *Mémoires*.

[2] The Fonds Suzanne de Diétrich (Suzanne de Diétrich Papers) was officially deposited in the Alsatian section of the National and University Library of Strasbourg on 23 February 1990. Thanks to the work of Thérèse Klipffel the miscellaneous material has been ordered and classified.

[3] SdD; this and the following quotations from a six-page manuscript, *Souvenirs*.

[4] Henri Mellon, "Les cinq sœurs (d'après les souvenirs de Teddy et Bicky Trew)", in the family magazine *Le Dietrich*, no. 4, 1989.

[5] L. Roerich, *Une famille noble d'Alsace*, Strasbourg, 1911. *De Dietrich: Le tricentenaire*, a symposium of historical essays under the direction of Jean Pierre Kintz, Schiltigheim, 1986. H. Georger-Vogt, "Table généalogique", *ibid.*, pp.201-206. Short essays on the de Dietrich family and company have been published in the family magazine *Le Dietrich*, Niederbronn, since 1988. Issue 5, 1990, is totally devoted to SdD.

[6] This and the following quotation from SdD, *Souvenirs*, p.6.

2
A Turning Point

When the decision was taken for Suzanne to become an engineer, she was puzzled. She clearly remembered that moment: "I was thoughtful as I returned to my study and looked at the river. I had dreamed of Greek and Latin, of classical studies. But the essential thing was to get out. My uncle wanted to find a successor for my father. Apparently the idea to make me an engineer came to him already when I was still a little girl."[1]

This change of direction marked the whole of Suzanne's life with a troubling inner tension. Her longing to study the classics crystallized in the study and meditation on mainly one classical document, the Bible. Her study of engineering equipped her with a clarity of thought and a down-to-earth perspective which gave her teaching and writing a very special character when she became a biblical theologian.

A girl in a boy's school

For the first time in her life Suzanne had to go to a school. A problem immediately arose: Where could a girl prepare for studying engineering? In France it was impossible at that time. Suzanne's uncle would have liked her to go to the university in Zurich, but technical high-schools in German-speaking Switzerland where she could have prepared for university did not accept girls. The technical high-school of Lausanne was a possibility. Two engineers of the de Dietrich factories coached her for the entrance exam, one in algebra, the other in technical drawing.

Suzanne remembered "a winter of very hard work. Good-bye, classics! At Easter 1907 I passed the entrance exams for the technical high-school in Lausanne and was accepted, but only on condition that I reached an average mark of 8 out of 10." This seemed an impossible condition. The first test in descriptive geometry was a disaster: Suzanne could not understand the problem she had to solve and received a 1, simply for being present. A Polish class-mate gave her a few private lessons and in the next test she got an 8. Her initial failure became part of the school's oral tradition. "The following year pupils whispered in the corridors: 'This is a terribly difficult test; Suzanne got a 1!'"

Her recollections continued: "I never had anything to complain about in my school-mates. They were very friendly and our relationship was almost as if I had been a boy." In her letters of the time Suzanne gives graphic descriptions of her teachers, who must have been an interesting and competent team. She remembers this period of two and a half years in the high-school as a happy one. At the end of the trial year her average mark was over 9. Together with a boy she came out at the top of her class in the baccalaureate.

Today it is hard to imagine how extraordinary it was in 1906 for a girl to prepare for studies in engineering. Suzanne's uncle and legal guardian, Baron Eugène de Dietrich, had no prejudices in this respect. He had detected the intelligence of his brother's little daughter, and he was keen to keep control of the de Dietrich business in the family.

As a child Suzanne had already learned the Greek alphabet. The books she read as a teenager point to her interest in classics, philosophy and the social sciences. Yet when the decision was made with regard to her future, she plunged with determination into the world of mathematics. Her earliest extant letters are full of ciphers, geometry and problems of algebra. They were addressed to Marguerite Ecoffey who was four and a half years older and who had just started studying mathematics. The two became inseparable friends.

The girl who comes through these early letters is not an unmitigated intellectual. The discussion of a mathematical problem is followed by the poetic description of a landscape or girlish gossip. From the age of 16 on there are increasing signs of a new religious and social consciousness. The Christ of the stained-glass window in the church of Niederbronn who had been so close to the little girl now began to challenge the young woman in another way — through religious instruction given by a pastoral friend and the readings he suggested.

The conversion of a sceptic

Before going to Lausanne, Suzanne had to study for her confirmation. The Lutheran catechetical training in German had made little impact on her sisters, all of whom, with the exception of the oldest one, remained agnostics. Suzanne's religious instruction was therefore entrusted to Jules Breitenstein, pastor of the evangelical chapel in Strasbourg. At the time this was the only place in Alsace where worship and instruction were conducted in French. Suzanne later said that Breitenstein had exercised a decisive influence on her. "I was a sceptical young girl who asked a lot of questions. I owe it to him to have met Jesus Christ. As I neared the age of twenty there still were crises of doubt, but I came out of these more deeply rooted in a faith which was to become the strength of my life." In spite of initial hesitation, confirmation for Suzanne meant a conversion experience, a decisive turning point in her life. It took place in spring 1907, before she left for Lausanne. A letter of December 1908 describes another conversion experience. During a Christmas vacation in Wolfershoffen, she wrote to Marguerite: "My whole inner life has been in the process of fading out. I told myself that I would never be a Christian. I was irritable, complaining, even more egoistic than usual and deeply unhappy each time I withdrew into myself. I was without strength, and felt lost. Then suddenly came peace. I am not a better person now, but I feel I am saved. The load which oppressed me has disappeared. Doubts, uncertainty and a faith which I had kept up only through an effort of will and which I knew had a shaky foundation have given way to a certainty I had sought after for many months, the calm certainty Pascal writes about... The idea of salvation by grace alone had always shocked my reason and my understanding of human dignity, my independence; now I am forced to accept it, to give in to this fait accompli. On the one hand I now have the strength and peace of a child of God; on the other, I know I am perfectly unworthy and I have done nothing to deserve it. I do not know what has happened and I am too thankful to try and reason it out. No explanation satisfies me; I tend to believe in a mysterious intervention." [2]

This was only a beginning. As for most Christians, conversion became for Suzanne a life-long process of ups and downs, but a basic certainty and sense of direction had been given, and accepted. How was her life to continue?

Breitenstein: pastor, father, friend

The decision to entrust the religious instruction of the sceptical young Suzanne to such an intelligent and pastoral man as Breitenstein proved providential. Instead of indoctrinating her with fixed statements of faith, he let her read serious Christian literature and critically discussed it with her. During their time together in Niederbronn a relationship of mutual trust and respect developed between them. Suzanne could freely express her doubts and questions and she found herself understood and challenged. This dialogue continued in the correspondence between the two, starting in 1907.

Breitenstein was born in 1873 in Avully, near Geneva, the son of a primary school teacher from whom he inherited considerable pedagogic gifts. In 1895, soon after the World Student Christian Federation (WSCF) was founded at the castle at Vadstena in Sweden, he heard John R. Mott speak at the first Sainte-Croix conference of the Swiss Student Christian Movement (SCM). Breitenstein came under the spell of Mott's vision of a worldwide community of faith whose members witness to their common Lord and serve in all areas of life, and especially in universities.

After short periods of pastoral service in France, Breitenstein was ordained as a Reformed pastor in 1897, and became the chaplain of the evangelical free church in Strasbourg. There he served until 1907 when he responded to a call of the church in Satigny, a village near Geneva. He also began to teach New Testament courses at the free church seminary in Geneva. In 1910 he became a full-time professor, teaching at the free church seminary and the theological faculty of Geneva university. For a time he tried to combine his pastoral work in Satigny with his academic ministry, but this proved too heavy a load, all the more so because occasionally he was also called upon to teach New Testament at the faculty of the free church in Lausanne. Breitenstein thus moved from Strasbourg to the Geneva/Lausanne area in the same year Suzanne moved from Niederbronn to Lausanne. The beginning of his teaching ministry coincided with Suzanne's growing interest in the Bible.

Breitenstein's reading covered a wide area. As a preacher, speaker at youth conferences and writer of articles he was much in demand. All his life he remained basically a pastor, deeply committed to the biblical training of lay people. From a rather narrow evangelical milieu, he was averse to any dogmatic stance which allowed no honest questioning of the biblical text. He was well acquainted with the highly critical approach to biblical studies which had developed in Germany. As a teacher he followed the middle way where critical study served to question narrow dogmatic positions and at the same time helped to build up a sound Christian faith. Breitenstein became known to a wider public especially through his published short meditations. He wrote in a clear, elegant style, concentrating on basic biblical affirmations and challenging readers to think for themselves. Both Breitenstein's approach to the Bible and his way of writing became models for Suzanne.

It was shortly after the death of her father that Suzanne met her religious instructor. Almost inevitably her pastor became her ideal father image. In 1907 she wrote to her friend Marguerite: "I know only one man with whom

a woman could be perfectly happy, and this man is Mr Breitenstein."
When her friend teased her Suzanne responded: "I know a little of what
it means to take a fancy for someone. But the feeling I have for him is
basically quite different. It is the Christian I love in him rather than the
man whom in any case I hardly know; I love him like a father, a
master."[3]

Soon after Suzanne made this discerning analysis of her feelings she
spent four weeks in the same hotel as Mr and Mrs Breitenstein at Saas-
Fee. There she came to know her pastor as an ordinary human being. At
first this was a disappointment — he spent hours playing billiards and
bridge and had no time to talk to his adopted daughter! Breitenstein had
repeatedly warned Suzanne not to idealize him. Now, at Saas Fee, he
maintained a certain distance. This was probably not only because he
badly needed to relax and did not want to have endless theological
discussions, but also because of his great pastoral wisdom. It was perhaps
at his request that his very down-to-earth wife spent much time with
Suzanne during those weeks. And gradually Suzanne learned to appreciate not only the Christian but also the man.

The Christian heritage

Suzanne seldom spoke about her ancestors, yet among them were men
and women of great faith; for instance, in the seventeenth century
Dominique Dietrich and Marguerite, his courageous wife, and in the
nineteenth Suzanne's paternal grandparents, Baron Albert de Dietrich and
his wife Adélaïde. Having such ancestors now encouraged the converted
sceptic who was just beginning her own pilgrimage of faith.

Dominique Dietrich (1620-94) was the first famous member of the
Dietrich family. He was the mayor of Strasbourg who in 1681 signed the
treaty by which this city was attached to the kingdom of France.
Dominique had negotiated and obtained the assurance that the Lutherans
of Strasbourg could retain freedom of worship. This freedom had been
guaranteed since the Edict of Nantes in 1598, but even before the
revocation of this edict in 1685 strong pressure was put on prominent
Protestants to become Catholics. The absolute monarchy of Louis XIV
would not tolerate religious pluralism. Thus the leadership of Strasbourg,
and especially the highly esteemed Dominique Dietrich, became the
target of a conversion campaign. Dominique was relieved of his office
and summoned to Paris. He stood firm against all persuasion, although
twice he was sent into exile in predominantly Catholic regions of France.
Faced with such spiritual resistance, pressure was put on Dominique's

second wife, Marguerite Dietrich-Wencker. However, they had not reckoned with her strength of character; she also stood firm. In fact, twice she managed to get her husband back to Strasbourg. Afraid that during his exile opponents might spread the rumour that he had converted, Dominique wrote and sealed his own Lutheran confession of faith: "I, Dominique Dietrich of Strasbourg, attest before God Almighty, that I have assurance in soul and conscience, and I believe and recognize that the evangelical religion, the confession of Augsbourg, as kept in our church, is in conformity to the word of God who alone can give salvation. I have no doubt on this subject but on the contrary am devoted with heart and soul to this religion and resolved to remain firm in this belief for life and death..."[4] Suzanne did not follow the strongly Lutheran confessional stance of her ancestor, but his example was a source of strength to her.

Suzanne's grandfather, Albert de Dietrich (1802-88), carried the family business through the crisis years of 1847-51 and coped with the challenges of the nineteenth-century industrial revolution and the technological innovations that led to steady growth. It was he who introduced into the de Dietrich emblem the motto: *Non sibi, sed aliis,* "Not for oneself, but for others". Something of that spirit was reflected in the way the company was run in his day. As a youth Albert had visited the old pastor, educator and social reformer Jean-Frédéric Oberlin in Ban de la Roche, and Oberlin's vision and work had an impact on the de Dietrich factories. As early as 1827, a retirement fund for workers was set up. Thirty years later Baron Albert received a prize for his innovative social policies. He is remembered as a patriarchal figure, much solicited for leadership positions in politics and church affairs. Like his ancestor Dominique, he was a pious conservative Lutheran and, referring to Dominique's confession, he testified that "he too would not desert the divine word and law". On business trips he always carried his Bible and writings of Christian authors. His notebooks are a strange mixture of notes on business conversations, orders for factory products and summaries of sermons by revivalist preachers. After the early death of his first wife, Fanny Octavie von Stein, he married one of her sisters, Suzanne's grandmother Adélaïde von Stein. Together with her Albert kept up many links with the revival movements of the nineteenth century.

Adélaïde de Dietrich-von Stein had died long before Suzanne was born and Suzanne had no direct memories of her grandfather. However, what she had heard about their faith and Baron Albert's social concern must have left some impact on the converted sceptic, especially when she began to learn more about Oberlin and the succession of men and women

of great faith at Ban de la Roche. In fact they became Suzanne's spiritual
ancestors.

Ban de la Roche

"I consider my spiritual roots are in Ban de la Roche, that humble
corner of Alsace, the land of my ancestors. A strange breed of men
lived there, with an irenic spirit and a social awareness. Like Oberlin I
would like to call myself a 'reformed Catholic'."[5] This is how
Suzanne summed up her spiritual ancestry. The county of Ban de la
Roche in the high valley of Bruche has only eight villages and a few
hamlets. Suzanne once called this poor and isolated area the "origin of
French ecumenism".

Jean-Frédéric Oberlin (1740-1826) worked there with his wife and
some helpers for almost sixty years as pastor, educator and socio-
economic reformer. By enlarging roads and building bridges he opened
this area to the outside world. He raised the living standard of the poor
population through basic health care and the introduction of an industry
which would not alienate people from their land and family. He welcomed Baron Jean de Dietrich III as the new count of this earldom. The
mainly Protestant inhabitants were happy that the ownership had passed
from a Catholic overlord to a Protestant. But tensions did arise on
occasion. The intensive use of the ironworks in Rothau led to the over-
exploitation of the forests which endangered Oberlin's plans for development. Sharp letters were exchanged in 1788: Jean III, the "king of iron",
advised Oberlin to confine himself to "spiritual matters". The pastor then
reminded the baron that the God he served was the one to whom a de
Dietrich also had to account for his acts.[6] Suzanne was not proud of this
part of her family history. Despite such tensions, however, Ban de la
Roche became a refuge for persecuted noble families during the years of
the revolution.

Oberlin had been looking for someone who would come and develop
a cottage industry. A pious industrialist family from Basel, the Le
Grands, responded positively. The father, Jean-Luc Le Grand, had
worked with the great Swiss educator Heinrich Pestalozzi. He helped
Oberlin especially in the field of popular education. The son, Daniel Le
Grand (1783-1859), looked after the cottage industry of band weaving
and, after Oberlin's death, assumed much of his role in Ban de la Roche.
He anticipated much of the present labour legislation, especially concerning child labour and the exploitation of women in industry. He also called
for more justice through taxing the wealthier people.

The different ways of Dieterlen and Fallot

"I was struck by an excellent small brochure on prayer written by Christoph Dieterlen, an industrialist of Rothau. He concentrated totally on the kingdom of God and the church universal. My first Christian reading — I was then 17 years old — was Tommy Fallot, and later I assimilated Fallot's thinking through his disciple, Marc Boegner."[7] These two, Dieterlen and Fallot, symbolized for Suzanne two different ways of obedience, and for many years she wondered which one to follow.

Christoph Dieterlen (1818-75) was born in Alsace. In 1847 he became the associate, and soon also the son-in-law, of Gustave Steinheil, the new director of the factories in Rothau after the de Dietrichs had sold them. Dieterlen stayed there with his large family until Alsace was annexed by Germany in 1871. In his early thirties he met the German pastor Johann Christoph Blumhardt, the great spiritual leader of the revival in Möttlingen. Dieterlen kept in contact with Blumhardt and supported him financially in the purchase and development of Bad Boll as the spiritual centre of a special type of southern German pietism — a very realistic belief in the power of God, like that of the early Christians, closely linked with a deep concern for the affairs of this world and its destiny. While continuing his daily work as an industrialist Dieterlen became a pastoral friend to those in need. He had great gifts of sympathy, of suffering together with the poor for whom he was a prophet of hope. Through this Christian way of life he also became a unique Christian thinker and mystic. Upheld by the biblical vision of God's coming kingdom, he struggled in prayer against evil powers and for an all-embracing solidarity. Refusing to be bound by theological doctrines or Christian institutions, he concentrated on daily meditation on the Bible. His writings — a series of short brochures most of which were published without the author's name — are unsystematic biblical reflections on the human predicament. The key to his thought was the affirmation that all human beings are created in the image of God, this image which, now distorted in us, can be seen and met in Christ, the second Adam who remained in total solidarity with both God and all human beings. As Dieterlen thus related each person and all everyday events to the reality of the coming kingdom, he communicated to many a sense of the presence of God's invisible world.

Tommy Fallot (1844-1904) was born in Ban de la Roche. For many years he followed the example of Dieterlen whom he acknowledged as his spiritual master. He became a textile engineer, married a niece of Dieterlen, worked as a Christian industrialist, and was deeply involved in the social and educational services which had been started by Oberlin. Gradually he became convinced that he could best serve the people as a pastor. He studied theology, presented a thesis on "The poor and the gospel", and became the deputy pastor in Wildersbach, the poorest village in Ban de la Roche. By then he had been strongly influenced by north German pietism, British revivalism and the popular mission created in Paris by Mac All. Disagreeing with the Lutheran understanding of church-state relationship, especially the prescribed prayers for the German emperor, he left Alsace to become the minister of the free church chapel in Paris. There he became involved in the work of the popular mission. Along the lines of Josephine Butler's work in Great Britain he started the struggle against the exploitation of women in France, and he was among the first militant advocates of Christian socialism. Illness forced him to abandon these activities, and after years spent recovering and meditating he became a pastor of the Reformed church in isolated villages in the Drôme area of France. There he wrote his major works, among them a synthesis of Dieterlen's perception of Christian faith and his own, the *Livre de l'action bonne* (a summary of his theological and social thinking, posthumously published by his pupil and nephew Marc Boegner). This was one of the first Christian books Suzanne read.

Suzanne's own life and thought were deeply influenced by Fallot — and through him by his master Dieterlen and his disciple Boegner. That influence was pervasive, but the following elements are of particular importance.

Dieterlen and Fallot were nurtured by a study of the Bible in the context of daily life, a study unhampered by confessional and dogmatic presuppositions. Fallot saw, for instance, that the typical Protestant emphasis on the prophets of the Old Testament is one-sided and that the sacerdotal or priestly dimension of the biblical message must be kept together with the prophetic one. He attempted to see the total plan of redemption revealed in scripture, much as Suzanne later did much more explicitly.

Fallot, like his uncle Dieterlen and his grand-father Le Grand, had a strong social awareness. If Le Grand was the precursor of much of the work of the International Labour Office, Fallot helped to initiate and develop French Protestant social thinking and action. This led him to emphasize the role of ordinary Christians in their daily work and in society as a whole. No wonder that Suzanne later devoted so much time to biblical reflection on law and justice and that she became one of the pioneers of the ecumenical rediscovery of the role of the laity.

Fallot was an advocate for unity among French Protestants. Unlike Dieterlen he became involved in the institutional church, and struggled to build up from within a living body of believers. Moreover, he made his own Oberlin's hope to be a "reformed Catholic", and looked forward to the time when Protestants and Catholics would come together. Suzanne had the same passion for unity. And she saw what Fallot did not perceive, that the worship and tradition of the Orthodox churches could contribute greatly to such unity.

Suzanne's life was strongly influenced by the spirituality of Dieterlen and Fallot, whose centre was the cross and whose horizon was the coming of God's kingdom. While this spirituality remains down-to-earth, it also makes present the powers of God's invisible world through prayer and active waiting.

The fear of life

It was probably Breitenstein who brought to Suzanne's notice the writings of Dieterlen and Fallot. Her resolute turning to Christ in 1907-08 did not mean that all her scepticism and critical self-analysis had miraculously evaporated. In answer to Suzanne's long letters (unfortunately not preserved), Breitenstein advised her to read the social and religious studies of Gustave Frommel, a systematic theologian and apologist who had been his own teacher. For study he recommended the analysis of the religious experience by William James, books by the Swiss Christian socialists Hermann Kutter and Leonhard Ragaz, and French and German religious socialist journals. It was in the company of Breitenstein that "under the larch trees of Saas Fee" Suzanne read and discussed John Calvin, an author who never much attracted her. Earlier, however, she had read Blaise Pascal's *Pensées* which impressed her so much that she copied many pages of the book in her book of quotations. During these years, 1907-09, the works of a strange mixture of thinkers and writers appear in Suzanne's reading list. She attempted to get through a treatise on mathematics by Henri Poincaré. She read extracts from the works of Plato, Marcus Aurelius, Montaigne, Goethe, Victor Hugo, Vinet, Renan, Secrétan, Tolstoy, Ruskin, Stephenson and Kipling. There was also some lighter reading in between, including detective stories.

The insights she gained from Dieterlen and Fallot were reinforced by her reading of contemporary authors, and made Suzanne impatient with her studies. She wanted to become involved in the struggles of her time. She felt helpless and lonely. "Sometimes I have the fear of living."[8] It was at such moments of self-analysis and discouragement that Suzanne needed, and received, spiritual guidance from Breitenstein. Again and again he led her back to her present task: "The day will come when you will have to give yourself to the struggle; for the moment you must give yourself to preparing for it. It is good that you see yourself as you are, with all the shortcomings that distress you; but do not indulge too much in self-criticism. Look rather at the world where a great harvest waits for workers; look at him who so loved the whole of humanity, who loved you so much that he gave himself without reservation."[9]

NOTES

[1] SdD, this and the following quotations from *Mémoires*.
[2] SdD, letter of 28 December 1908 to Ecoffey.
[3] SdD, letters of 29 July 1907 and 19 July 1909 to Ecoffey.
[4] Full text in *De Dietrich: Le tricentenaire*, pp.25f.
[5] SdD, "Expériences œcuméniques", *Foi et vie*, 1960, p.178. Cf. SdD, "Le Ban de la Roche: berceau d'un œcuménisme français", *ibid.*, 1961, pp.27-34.
[6] *Le Dietrich*, no. 7, 1990. This whole issue is devoted to the relationship between the de Dietrichs and Ban de la Roche.
[7] SdD, "Expériences œcuméniques", p.178. On Le Grand, Dieterlen and Fallot, see Marc Boegner, *La vie et la pensée de T. Fallot*, vol. I, Paris, 1914; vol. II, Paris, 1926.
[8] SdD, letter of 15 August 1910 to Ecoffey.
[9] Breitenstein, letter of 21 June 1908 to SdD.

3
Drawing Board and Bible

"I worked extremely hard to get a diploma [in engineering] which I never used and I have not done enough study for what is now my work."[1] Looking back, that was how Suzanne described the paradox in her life.

A twin passion

In summer 1909 Suzanne was 18 and had just completed her baccalaureate in science. Her uncle wanted her to study in Zurich, but she successfully pleaded for the school of engineering attached to Lausanne university. It was not with any great enthusiasm that she started her studies. While waiting for the baccalaureate certificate she began reading a history of philosophy. She confessed that larch trees attracted her much more than the most impressive machines. No wonder the next three and a half years were mostly hard work for her. In her autobiographical notes she devotes only a few lines to her studies: "They were rather hard, these seven semesters. I had to stand for hours at the large drawing board. Each week there were forty-three hours at the school and frequent tests which quite often meant I had to work until three in the morning. I was very conscientious and very slow."[2]

During these packed months of studies Suzanne found little time for her correspondence. The long letters written during the vacations show how exhausted she was. "Have you ever dissected the brain of an overworked student?" she asked her friend Marguerite Ecoffey who had switched from mathematics to medical studies. "It must look quite odd, totally flattened convolutions." That was the way she often felt, but unlike several of her fellow students she never gave up or postponed exams. In 1913 she became the second woman in French-speaking Europe to complete her engineering studies successfully.

At the high-school Suzanne had been the only girl in her class. Now in the school of engineering two other women joined the group of eighty male students. Both came from eastern Europe, the one a Georgian who left after her first year, the other Lydia Menzinger, a Russian of Baltic

origin. Suzanne wrote about their relationship: "We discussed a great
deal together. She was an agnostic but open to ideas, and to my great
joy I saw her gradually opening herself to faith. I took her along to a
student Christian conference in Sainte-Croix and invited her into my
family." Twice Lydia spent several weeks with Suzanne and
Mademoiselle Boillot for hydrotherapy cures in Switzerland and Germany. Together they read the novels of Tolstoy, Dostoyevsky and other
Russian writers. In 1912 Lydia had to return to Moscow, but she
continued writing to Suzanne until 1920. In Moscow she became a
member of the then very pietist Russian SCM. During the war she
worked as a nurse in a psychiatric clinic. The letters from Suzanne must
have helped her to bridge the gulf between her individualistic and other-
worldly faith and her great socio-political aspirations. Lydia's letters
brought news of what was happening in Russia during those crucial
years. She belonged to the westernized Russian intelligentsia who
welcomed the February revolution of 1917 but were disappointed with
the October 1917 events. She and her family were probably all killed. In
her last letter she wrote: "Despite all the difficulties I feel utterly happy,
for I have definitely found the Christ who was seeking me for many
years. Since the autumn of 1919 I have been a soldier of the Salvation
Army, for it is there where Jesus revealed himself to me as my Saviour
and God."

Another young woman who made a great impact on Suzanne's life
was Renée Warnery, a Swiss medical student whom she met in
Lausanne in 1909. "She had a soul of fire," Suzanne recalled. "She
had come to know the World Student Christian Federation in England
and she stirred up enthusiasm among her French-Swiss compatriots.
Later she became a convert to Catholicism. She died young, leaving us
with the memory of a warm heart, an indomitable will and a fine
intelligence." It was Warnery who introduced Suzanne to group Bible
study which had developed in the British SCM. She invited her to
become a member of the SCM in Lausanne and encouraged her to take
on its leadership during the academic year 1910-11. Students from all
university faculties met regularly to study the Bible and discuss their
own and the world's problems. The meeting, "Saturday afternoon
recreation" as she once called it, became in fact her spiritual home. It
was also the first training ground for what would become her life-long
ministry. She characterized these years as the time of her "twin
passions", studies at the school of engineering and the student
association.

Study groups and student foyers

Her enthusiasm for student work started when in the autumn of 1909 Suzanne received permission from her uncle ("if Mademoiselle Boillot agrees") to attend the Sainte-Croix student conference. For the first time in her life Suzanne lived for a few days with a group of like-minded young people without the caring — and hampering — presence of Boillot or any other member of the family. The pietistic style of the early Sainte-Croix conferences was being challenged by some young leaders, among them Warnery, who pleaded for a less dogmatic approach to the Bible and greater intellectual honesty. During the following years Suzanne went several times to these autumn Sainte-Croix conferences, which were mainly periods of retreat and renewal for Christian students. Agnostics and seekers rarely attended them. That was why spring conferences were started in La Sarraz, near Lausanne, which took up general questions of student life and where the large number of foreign students felt more at home.

Before the first world war more than half the students in Swiss universities were foreigners, in Geneva almost eighty percent. The majority came from Eastern Europe, among them many women who often lived in deplorable conditions. In 1906 John R. Mott's colleague in the WSCF, Ruth Rouse, visited Swiss universities and urged the local SCMs to open places to welcome these women students, promising support for the project from Anglo-Saxon movements. In 1909 Elisabeth Clark from the USA, with local support, opened such a "welcome room" near the university in Geneva. Shortly afterwards a similar "foyer" was also started in Lausanne with the help of Annette Tritton from Great Britain. Suzanne immediately became part of the small Christian team which animated the life of this foyer where foreign women students, many of them agnostics, met.

In the gatherings of both the Lausanne SCM and the foyer Suzanne was sometimes asked to speak. She felt quite inadequate for this task. "I promised myself not to preach to people until I had put my own life a little more in order in accordance with my principles," she wrote to her friend. "I want the SCMs to be a movement of friendship, as Mott talked about."[3] Only a person like Warnery, she felt, had the authority to speak about Christian faith to outsiders. Suzanne detested all talk about conditions for SCM membership and the rules on who could or could not become a member. She pleaded for an open group where deeply committed Christians would attempt to *live* their faith among fellow students and so serve the missionary purpose of the WSCF. Despite the reluctance to confess her faith openly, Suzanne became gradually convinced that speaking to groups was one of her gifts which she should use. In 1910 she made a presentation to the Lausanne SCM on the British art historian John Ruskin. Two years later she was asked to be one of the main speakers at the spring conference in La Sarraz.

A talk which caused Suzanne much soul-searching was the Christmas message she was asked to give at the foyer in 1913. She described the fears and joys of that experience in one of her letters. She had shared her carefully prepared notes with Mademoiselle Boillot, as she often did when she had to give a talk. Yet as the moment came near she felt she could not find the right words and she panicked. Meanwhile at the foyer Bulgarian, Polish, Russian and German students were already gathering. "We always sat in a circle, gossiping and laughing. I had the impression of coming with my religious talk like a cold shower, catching them off guard; you know how I hate this. Then I took my courage in both hands and plunged into it, and suddenly it went all right. The sentences came by themselves and I hardly looked at my notes... 'When I am weak, then I am strong.'"[4] Suzanne spoke about Christmas as a message of social justice. She presented Christ as a companion on the way, a friend in whose company one finds the power to struggle for justice and peace and with whom the struggle becomes a joy.

Besides giving lectures and meditations, Suzanne began to develop her very special gift for Christian teaching and testimony: leading participatory Bible studies in small groups. From 1910 on she started reading biblical commentaries. Breitenstein provided her with bibliographies and gave her some good advice on how to lead such studies. Among the commentaries she consulted were the heavy German exegetical volumes of Johannes Weiss and Adolf Deissmann. Suzanne's first written Bible study outline comes from that summer of 1911 and deals with the passion story in Mark's gospel. She submitted it to her pastoral friend who found it excellent, and suggested further readings to her.

In the SCM Suzanne had met theological students who were following Breitenstein's New Testament courses on Paul's letter to the Galatians and on the apostolic period. She borrowed their notes and during the summer months studied them carefully together with the notes from her exegetical readings. During vacation time the Bible definitely won over the drawing board. She wrote to Ecoffey: "I have had wonderful hours with the apostles, especially Paul. They are so full of life, so full of energy." No wonder Paul became her hero; she recognized herself in him. His difficult character, his self-examination and his thorn in the flesh constantly reminded her of her own experiences. Like Paul she had to learn to live by grace alone.

Prophets of life

Summer 1913: Suzanne obtained her diploma in engineering. What was she to do now? Should she follow Christoph Dieterlen, and serve as a Christian in industry? Or Tommy Fallot, and concentrate on building a mature Christian community? She was at a crossroads. Even Breitenstein wondered whether work in the de Dietrich company should really be Suzanne's way of service; he had early detected her special gift for writing. Then he read Suzanne's address at the La Sarraz student conference in 1912 which had just been published. That marked a turning point: their father-daughter relationship developed into a friendship of equals, committed to the same cause. He wrote about her lecture: "I feel that you have written these pages in the presence of God. Now I know more than ever that you will be a power for the cause, as the old Huguenots used to say, that your pen will be a weapon and that you will be able to preach without a pulpit and chapel." Later he summed up their common task: "Always to be a sower of hope and a prophet of life."

That first published address of Suzanne, then 21 years old, could have been entitled: "Prophets of Life". Asked to speak on "What does it mean to be saved?", she answered with just two words: "to live". [5] That might have shocked students from pietistic backgrounds. Instead of the traditional salvation language, here was something based on scientific observation and everyday human experience. Scientists can only establish the presence of physical life; they cannot define its mystery. The same is true of believers; they cannot explicate the mystery of spiritual life. To judge the worth of a tree one must look at its fruit, as Jesus did with his eminently experimental method of teaching. True believers are like true scientists.

Those who explore the mysteries of the physical world and those who seek to understand the secrets of the spiritual life discover only very small parts of what they are looking for. They can only stand in humility before the infinity of truth. Only pseudo-scientists and complacent Christians will lay claim to knowledge in all its fullness.

Christ did not expound a doctrine of salvation. He helped people to become a hearth, "a 'foyer' of divine and free life through communion with the living God". In the light of that conviction, Suzanne simply presented materials for building up faith, based on "some personal experiences". Her words indeed had the authority of "lived truth", of a struggle for life. She spoke of her spiritual journey in such a way that it did not become an individual testimony, typical of revival meetings, but a more objective, verifiable analysis of life. To a certain degree the hearers could recognize in it part of their own experience and aspirations.

How does salvation relate to life? According to Suzanne a germ of divine life is present in each person, but the repeated failure to follow one's conscience leads to a vague fear of life. Believers of all ages have cried: "I am lost", from Isaiah and Paul to Francis of Assisi, Pascal and our own times. Those who never made an attempt to live in the presence of the living God may explain this feeling of guilt as a pathological phenomenon. But under the empty heaven they themselves are often led to a "disgust of life", bringing cynicism and self-destruction. The germ of divine life can grow and bear fruit if we are in union with Christ, who is the image of true humanity. We then recognize ourselves in him, not as we are now but as we are meant to become and want to become. This Christ "is not the Christ of the churches' stained-glass windows, with a halo. It is the man who could silence the accusers of the adulterous woman; who could denounce the pious people of his time as whitewashed tombs because they left widows and orphans without support; who, with gentleness and infinite tenderness, took care of the poor human wrecks he met on his way; who could comfort and strengthen his frightened disciples." The closer we come to this Christ, the more we learn to live and the emptiness of our life becomes filled with love.

This does not happen through any magical transformation. Christ is a Saviour who works with us. While we cannot save ourselves, neither can we remain totally passive. Forgiveness has to be accepted, and we must strive towards the conversion of our will. Here Suzanne dared to take up the difficult question of determinism and free will. She acknowledged that all of us are to a great extent determined by our heredity and our milieu, but she refused to accept any irreducible opposition between the reason which speaks in favour of determinism and the conscience which affirms a free will. She therefore insisted that our primary task is to be seekers of truth with total sincerity. As we recognize on that search our true being in Christ we also hear his call to follow him. This takes us on a way we do not want to take. Jesus has made clear what it entails: Whoever wants to be my disciple let him take up his cross. "What is at stake here is not a belief in the sacrifice of Christ but a belief in the universal law of sacrifice, in the divine law of solidarity and love. Jesus is powerful because he has given himself: through death to life." Suzanne argued from what can be observed in nature itself, where the grain must die in order to bear fruit. She also lifted up our own search for salvation to the realm of God's universal plan. As on the way of discipleship Christ begins to live in us "our individual salvation will no more appear to us as an aim but as a means. The aim is the salvation of the world." In response to God's amazing act of faith in humanity we cannot but go ahead and become humble sowers of life. "To be saved means to have an invincible certainty that God will *win*, in us and in the world."

Not many of the participants at the conference knew that almost every sentence of that talk had been lived and experienced by the speaker. Her presentation was of course full of insights which she had gained from Pascal, Dieterlen, Fallot and Breitenstein, but these insights had been tested in her own life and become existentially her own. For Suzanne the ultimate purpose of her life was now clear, but she still stood undecided at the crossroads, wondering which way to choose to move towards that goal.

In the whirlpool

"I am a badly put together old carriage," wrote Suzanne to her friend Ecoffey, summarizing the verdict of her latest medical examination, but she continued confidently: "As long as the head is good, forget about the legs; I must cycle, ride on horses, drive in cars, whatever I want. Above all, nobody is to pester me any longer with diets, cures and massages. They must let me live like everybody else. In other words: nothing can be done to change me, so let me enjoy what I have." Suzanne tried to do exactly this. For once she did not have to submit to another hydro-therapeutic cure during the summer vacation of 1913 and she thought, quite mistakenly, that she was finally out of the hands of physicians. She spent that summer in Alsace where she could go on long cycling tours and for walks with her visitors. Amélie Trew-de Dietrich had come from Canada with her family and Suzanne liked her nephews. Soon, however, she began to long for intellectual stimulation and city life. At times she felt like a stranger who had come on a visit. Then there were moments when she felt tempted to stay at home and work as an engineer. At the same time she confided to Ecoffey: "I have the strange impression that my future is already quite decided, that it no longer depends on me; and though I know nothing of what awaits me I have an increasingly clearer perception that it will not be here."

Suzanne's readings during that summer show how many different futures she explored. Heavy German Bible commentaries competed with large volumes of the history of modern France. Dostoyevsky, Tolstoy and the plays of Henrik Ibsen continued to fascinate her, but she also turned again to a mathemathical essay by Poincaré. In between she read a history of Alsace written for children, the novels of Flaubert, and a life of Leonardo da Vinci. In 1912 Suzanne had started to write a novel, which she soon abandoned. Now a quite different writing project occupied much of her time: a book on the feminist question. She collected information about the situation of women of different social classes, read literature on the suffragettes and, like Fallot, became deeply interested in the thought and action of Josephine Butler. The new interest was partly because she had an invitation, as yet unofficial, to attend a world YWCA conference in Stockholm. That summer she inherited from an aunt the "Schlössel", a large house which she decided to make available to the parish of Niederbronn for deaconesses who took care of patients among the poor. Thus one of her dearest dreams began to come true: a free clinic for working-class families.

From her uncle Suzanne had received permission to spend an additional year at the university of Geneva; she wanted to follow some of Breitenstein's courses. Warnery, who had recently moved to Geneva, had written enthusiastically about Prof. Flournoy's courses on Freud's theory of psychoanalysis. Suzanne also hoped to learn more about social questions and the industrial revolution. In the autumn of 1913 she took up residence in Geneva, still accompanied by Mademoiselle Boillot and a maid called Mary.

Even before the university semester started Suzanne joined the Geneva SCM, and was immediately asked to lead Bible study groups. She also became involved with the work among foreign women students at the foyer, and she volunteered to help part-time in the social welfare office. There Suzanne realized that to be effective in social service she needed to know more about the relevant legislation. But was it right for her to fritter away her time and talents on too many things? Should she not rather concentrate on one interest, the study of law, for example? Somewhat reluctantly she decided for the latter. Instead of learning Greek she now took private lessons in Latin, and for several weeks audited courses on Roman law. Then, much to her relief, she was told that with her science background she could not become a regular student in the law faculty.

The door was open for the strange mixture of courses which she followed during that winter semester of 1913-14: New Testament, psychoanalysis, the history of the industrial revolution, philosophy and some Greek! In addition there were extra-curricular activities: Suzanne had to prepare for leading group Bible studies on the gospels of John and Mark. There were daily visits to and from foreign women students. An SCM study circle on non-Christian religions wanted her to introduce a session on Buddhism — which annoyed her no end because of the necessarily superficial input at such study groups. She continued to work on feminism. Twice she made presentations on this subject in the foyer and was promptly accused of being an anti-feminist, because she dwelt more on the duties of women in society than on their rights. Following the advice of her doctors she also took riding lessons.

Such hectic and often unfocused activity might have been partly caused by the fact that Suzanne was facing an emotional crisis. For fifteen years the faithful Boillot had shared her work and vacations, her friendships and frustrations. Boillot's whole life centred on that small girl who had now grown into a 23-year old woman. This situation was soon to come to an end, but they each felt very differently about it. "For her", Suzanne wrote, "it is a life which ends; for me it is a life which is only just beginning. Everything looks beautiful to me and sad to her: I see only my vocation, she sees only the separation." [6]

Yet another bond showed signs of weakening — Suzanne's intimate friendship with Marguerite Ecoffey. It had started in 1907 when she was a student at the technical high-school and had found a warm welcome in the stable, bourgeois Ecoffey family. Marguerite, the second daughter of that hospitable home, had become her closest friend. Suzanne loved and idealized her, and the two spent most Sundays together. Now the younger girl was more sought after, and it was Marguerite who admired Suzanne. When they joined the Lausanne SCM, Suzanne was chosen as a leader. She had found a firm purpose for life in the Christian faith, but not Marguerite. Suzanne had obtained her diploma in engineering while Marguerite was still a medical student. In her internships in hospitals Marguerite was finding it difficult to develop human contacts with her patients.

Now Suzanne lived in Geneva and her world was expanding. She had not only listened from afar to the giants in the Christian student world of that time: J.R. Mott, Ruth Rouse and Robert P. Wilder. In a small group in Geneva she had opened her heart to Mott and discussed her hopes with him. In the Lausanne foyer mutual respect had grown between Suzanne and Annette Tritton. Work in the Geneva foyer led to an even deeper spiritual relationship with Clark's assistant, Constance Grant from New Zealand. The Geneva SCM brought Suzanne into contact with Philippe de Vargas who was preparing for missionary service in China, and with

Emmanuel Galland and his fiancée Yvonne van Berchem who were going to South America and who would become close friends. Meanwhile the official invitation for the forthcoming world YWCA conference in Stockholm had come, and Suzanne was to be not just a participant but one of the main speakers. Though Geneva is not far from Lausanne, Marguerite felt increasingly left behind in her small world by her friend who — as she admiringly, if grudgingly, wrote — was "in the process of becoming a famous woman". The two continued to write to and visit each other; in 1916-17 Marguerite even stayed for seven months in the same apartment with Suzanne in Paris, but despite mutual affirmations of love and friendship their ways were separating. For Marguerite this must have been a great sorrow. Nevertheless, it was in her letters to Marguerite (more than 260 written between 1907 and 1939) that Suzanne spontaneously shared her hopes and fears.

The road to follow

Suzanne's indecision came to a sudden end when in February 1914 she attended the national congress of the French SCM in Lyons and heard the plea of its general secretary, Charles Grauss: "We have received urgent appeals for help from Canada, the Orient, the Latin countries in Europe, the Balkans and especially from South America. Never shall we forget the welcome received from the South American delegates who pleaded with us to come and help them." Reporting on a WSCF world conference Grauss spoke with the fire of both Christian faith and French nationalism, making an appeal for faith, men and money. "Men: they are among us and will stand up because they cannot do otherwise."[7]

The speaker probably did not notice the small woman listening to him with rapt attention. He asked for men and he got a woman. Suzanne wrote to Marguerite from Lyons: "Listening to the report of Grauss I decided to enter the service of the French SCM from next autumn. I cannot tell you the emotion of that moment when I no longer had any doubt about which way to follow." Suzanne volunteered for two years and took up contact with Raoul Allier and Mrs Jacques Pannier, the president and vice-president of the French SCM. Grauss invited her to attend the Pentecost retreat of the Paris SCM at Versailles in order to get acquainted with the students and staff with whom she would be working.

It was not easy to write about this decision to her uncle and guardian. Baron Eugène made no objection, though he was not happy. With a clear conscience Suzanne could now decline the invitation which had come for leading the foyer in Lausanne. She had had enough of the Swiss bourgeois milieu and traditional Protestantism. Contacts with Warnery had helped her to see Catholicism in a new light, and meetings with Orthodox students awoke a desire to know more about the Eastern Christian tradition. Moreover, her readings on Buddhism had opened her mind to other religious dimensions. In the midst of her hectic activities she now spent a week of silent meditation in the company of Grant. After reading a biography of St Augustine she sometimes longed to be in a monastery (not a convent, because she had been told that she might find only a few books or none at all!). As a result of this longing for silence she cancelled a visit to Great Britain planned for the summer of 1914. After the Stockholm conference she planned to go to northern Sweden to spend some weeks of quiet preparation for her future ministry.

Stockholm, in June 1914, was the first of a long series of international Christian conferences for Suzanne. But she felt more at home in small groups and in meetings which provided opportunities for unhurried personal conversations. She was convinced that true humanity matures best in the complementarity of women and men, ideally in a good marriage and family. No wonder Stockholm did not greatly appeal to her.

But Suzanne had prepared thoroughly for her lecture on "The Civic Duties of Women" at Stockholm. She presented two theses: "(1) The emancipation of women is necessary from three points of view: juridical, economic and political. (2) This emancipation, a consequence of the principles expounded by Christ centuries ago, must be realized in the spirit of Christ if it is to become truly liberating." [8] Suzanne substantiated her first thesis with a wealth of information and statistics from all over the world, showing that "feminism is not a passing wave but a great flood tide whose irresistible flow carries the whole of society to as yet unknown new shores". What she said in her second thesis might not have pleased all the feminists: "It is not the fact that women will have the vote that will change the world, but the fact that they take seriously their social responsibility." Suzanne distinguished between two concepts of "equality". One she described as being that of those "demagogues" who seek, contrary to nature, to level out all differences, "resulting in a universal mediocracy". She herself advocated an equality which was "that of Christ, who wants the free blossoming of all according to their specific nature and limits. If the woman of tomorrow is to accomplish her mission she has to remain a woman above all."

In her letters from Stockholm Suzanne wrote at greater length about a small international girls camp where she led a Bible study than about the big conference. The spirit of prayer among both participants and leaders of that camp impressed her deeply: a good preparation for her Swedish "retreat" in a lonely corner of Jämtland. For the first time she now travelled alone: "Nobody worries about me or makes a fuss over me. What peace!"

NOTES

[1] Marc Chambron, interview with SdD, 20 August 1971, transcript p.3.

[2] SdD, this and the following quotations from *Mémoires*, pp.3f.

[3] SdD, letter of 20 September 1910 to Ecoffey.

[4] SdD, letter of 29 December 1912 to Ecoffey.

[5] SdD, *Qu'est-ce qu'être sauvé?*, Lausanne, 1912; this and following quotations from pp.3,5,15,17,19f.

[6] SdD, letter of 19 March 1914 to Ecoffey.

[7] Charles Grauss, "Trois dates", *Le semeur*, March 1914, pp.181 and 184.

[8] SdD, this and the following quotations from "Les devoirs civiques de la femme", *World YWCA Monthly*, 1914, pp.187,189,193f.

4
Testing Her Vocation

On 28 June 1914, a fatal gunshot in Sarajevo provoked a tense situation in central Europe. Suzanne was on her way to the north of Sweden, suspecting nothing. A month later, when war broke out, she was still lying in her hammock enjoying the peace of Jämtland. With some difficulty a Swedish peasant woman managed to make her understand that Germany had declared war on Russia and France.

There she was, on her first international trip alone, far from home. And where was home anyway? The Geneva flat had been vacated. Pro-French Alsatians had escaped westwards to fight for France and to liberate their German-occupied region. In Paris Suzanne had as yet no place to live, nor did she have a French passport. After days of travelling she reached Denmark. Her telegram to her uncle, enquiring whether she should attempt to return to Reichshoffen, had still not been answered. The French consul in Copenhagen gave her an entry permit to France. With some stranded French nationals she was evacuated to England, and from there sent to France. But members of the French SCM staff, with whom she had hoped to work, had already gone to the front.

The following years sorely tested Suzanne's vocation. In 1920 she wrote: "Who could have foreseen the moral disarray the war has caused in us — precisely because of the power of the religious and social dreams which had animated us in our youth? As members of the World's Student Christian Federation, disciples of the first apostles of Christian socialism, we had that very strong sense of human solidarity which is the new feature of this century. Full of wonderful dreams about international brotherhood and Christian unity we set out, young and cheerful, to conquer the world... We woke up with weapons in our hands."[1]

The early "Fédé"
Suzanne's life and work, from then till 1935, were closely linked with the French SCM. As in other parts of the world, in France too the SCM grew out of the French YMCA and YWCA, founded respectively in 1852

and 1894. A student YMCA group met in Paris from 1892. It became the Paris Association of Protestant Students, and it was strongly characterized by a revivalist spirituality, combined with early Christian socialism and a strong intellectual orientation. Similar groups soon developed in other French university centres, visited in 1898 by John R. Mott. It was partly due to him that in the same year the French Federation of SCMs was formed and accepted as a member of the WSCF, together with the Swiss and Dutch SCMs. While the Paris association emphasized its explicitly Protestant character, the French Federation sought to be a non-confessional Christian movement, ecumenically open though essentially Protestant, but without any official relationship with the churches.

The "Fédé" — as the French SCM is generally called — remained a small but influential movement. Up to 1920 its chairman and main spokesman was Raoul Allier, a philosopher and theologian who was professor at the Protestant theological faculty in Paris and taught at the Sorbonne as well. Through his many social and missionary involvements he had become an internationally well-known figure. Suzanne and most of her friends, however, were much more influenced by Charles Grauss. Born in 1881 in Alsace, he had studied commerce and law, and in 1906 became the general secretary of the Fédé. He was delighted with Suzanne's decision to join the SCM staff, but they never had the chance to work together because in August 1918 Grauss was killed in battle. Nevertheless, to the end of her life Suzanne felt a deep sense of companionship with this remarkable man.

The Fédé owed a great deal to its annual congresses and to the first French student journal, *Le semeur*. The journal carried daringly critical articles on socio-political questions, culture, theology and ethics, and it influenced the thinking and orientation of many future Protestant leaders in church and society. Pentecost retreats in Versailles for the Paris association and summer camps in Domino on the island of Oléron for the whole Fédé became annual training events. Soon a women's branch developed, as well as work among high-school students with their own periodical, *Notre revue*. In 1914 only about 400 men students were involved in the movement, together with about 300 women students and 450 members of the high-school branch, but despite these small numbers, the strong links of friendship, the quality of leadership and the loyalty of former members together turned the movement into the training ground of a French Protestant elite.

In Anglo-Saxon countries the SCM often grew out of student volunteer movements for foreign missions. In France the development was the other way round: a movement of "volunteers for Christ" grew out of the Fédé in 1913. These volunteers were male students and graduates from different university faculties who committed their life to full-time Christian service for the evangelization of the world. The founder, Francis Monod, had originally considered a missionary presence in Muslim countries, but later the volunteers began to think also in terms of evangelization among exploited factory workers and miners in the north of France, poor peasants in isolated mountain areas and the secularized students in the Latin quarter of Paris. Monod was killed in the first weeks of the war, and Grauss became the leading spirit. At the Lyons congress he made an impassioned appeal to young men to become heralds of Christ. During the next four years, however, their place of witnessing would be in the army and on the battle-fields.

Volunteers for Christ in the war

"Here the earth trembles from morning to evening, but each night there are beautiful stars in the sky," wrote Grauss in a note for Suzanne from the trenches. It expressed something of what the group of volunteers for Christ experienced during the war. Through her ever-welcoming presence in Paris when they were on leave, her intercession and correspondence, Suzanne shared this experience with them. A relationship of confidence and mutual support grew between her and several of these volunteers. Their letters from the front, hastily written in the trenches on small pieces of paper, form a moving human document. Suzanne used to say that besides the Bible these letters became her *viaticum* during the war. Her own letters to these officers, on active duty or recovering from wounds in military hospitals, proved to be a great source of comfort and support. [2]

The first thing one notices in this correspondence is the strong spirit of patriotism and the conviction that France was fighting for a just cause. Contrary to what happened in the British SCM, there was no movement of conscientious objection. Several times Suzanne wrote that she would have liked to be a man in order to join her friends in the battle. When she finally found a room in a student hostel in the Latin quarter she bought reproductions of art-work showing the four persons who became her "saints": Christ on the cross, Saint Geneviève, the patron saint of Paris, Jeanne d'Arc, and Rouget de l'Isle. Like her friends she believed that this struggle was a war against war, and she rejoiced when Grauss wrote to her from Verdun that he had seen birds from Alsace flying over the battle-field unafraid of the canons. "I joyfully returned to my machine guns, these labourers of death which work for peace."

Suzanne and her friends were convinced of the justice of their cause, but they tried to guard against hating the Germans. This soon led to conflict. In his weekly religious-patriotic speeches and his articles in *Le semeur* Allier insisted on the absolute responsibility of Germany for the war. Suzanne began a campaign against this view, starting with the WSCF World Day of Prayer in February 1915, in which she included prayers for German students in the army. She had long conversations with Mott when he passed through Paris in 1914 and 1916, and she also kept up her correspondence with Swiss friends. Through them she could occasionally communicate with her sister Marie in Germany, and she regularly wrote to her sisters in North America. She was in touch with de Vargas in China, the Gallands in South America, and Lydia Menzinger in Moscow. In March 1917 Lydia wrote enthusiastically about the Russian revolution: "What wonderful days we are living through! Our most daring dreams have come true. God heard the fervent prayers of millions for the salvation of our country. The great resurrection has happened in a miraculous way." But a few months later she was deeply disappointed about developments in her country.

Suzanne passed on all such information from the outside world to her friends on the front. Some of them saw in the February revolution in Russia a great turning point in history. Thus Alex de Faye wrote in spring 1917: "The deep meaning of what is happening is beginning to be apparent. The right word for the hour has been spoken by Grauss. Evaluating the events in Russia he ended by saying 'The war is really becoming holy.' Yes, it *is becoming* holy. The turn of events was difficult. It was hard to get rid of the old leaven of imperialism. Now it is really a democratic thrust surging forward to the walls of the German fortress." But this hope of real change was soon shattered. Suzanne and her friends then put their expectations for a lasting and just peace in the initiatives of the American president Woodrow Wilson.

In February 1916 Suzanne herself became a volunteer for Christ. During the congress in Lyons she had attended the volunteers' special meeting and decided that she would work for the creation of a parallel movement among women students and graduates. She heard that Martha Gourhan, a former SCM member who worked as a nurse, had already made her commitment as a volunteer. Others were praying for such a movement. In the name of this group Suzanne therefore wrote to Allier, telling him of the creation of the movement for women volunteers and asking permission to announce this at the meeting of the World Day of Prayer. She added the proposed formulation of commitment: "In response to a call which I have received, I commit myself to devote my life exclusively to the service of Christ and the furtherance of God's kingdom. Thus I resolve to put myself totally at the disposal of agencies of evangelization, be it in France or overseas. In all circumstances which could lead to a change of direction in my life, I commit myself to seek humbly God's will and to obey it."[3] Not everyone appreciated this *fait accompli*, but in the course of the next years a small number of women joined the movement. Suzanne made enquiries about service opportunities for women evangelists with academic training. She negotiated with social service agencies of the churches and with the leaders of the popular mission that the social thinker and evangelist Mac All had founded and with which Tommy Fallot had collaborated. Her great dream was to send a team of women doctors and nurses to Muslim countries overseas. In all this she was strongly supported by the volunteers at the front, especially by Grauss who said repeatedly that after the war the main burden of work and witness would have to be carried by women.

A sacrificial view of life was at the very centre of the commitment of the volunteers for Christ. However, as the war progressed, and after the indescribable horrors of such battles as Verdun and the Somme, the volunteers spoke less and less about sacrifice — they lived it. About one-fifth of the male members of the student and high-school branches of the Fédé were killed during the war. In their letters to Suzanne several volunteers wrote about their increasing desire to hear no more rhetoric on sacrifice and patriotism, but to find time to rethink their faith and commitment. As officers coming from an intellectual background they came to have an increasing respect for the courage, common sense and deep humanity of their soldiers, ordinary French workers and farmers. This challenged the elitism of the pre-war Fédé. Among Catholics and free thinkers they discovered the same hopes and commitments as their own, and it challenged their Protestant confessionalism.

The understanding of evangelism also changed. Referring to his relationship with the soldiers, Grauss wrote in 1917: "I never speak to them about the gospel, but I attempt to speak to them like the gospel, in their language and putting myself in their place." Such a conception of evangelism questioned the earlier and more militant ways of witnessing. This led later to heated debates among the volunteers: some wanted to stick to their original commitment to full-time service in church organizations or foreign mission; others asked whether the whole of Christian life was not meant to be a full-time witness, whatever one's profession. Suzanne never went back on her original commitment, but she now acknowledged that "to be simply a Christian" was enough. She saw the need to take the apostolate of the laity far more seriously. In the 1920s she therefore pleaded for the enlargement of the group of volunteers, including also members committed to witness in secular professions. Behind the questioning among the volunteers was a new confrontation with the Christian faith. A much greater sense of realism and indeed a new understanding of Christ now began to emerge: no longer the conquering, triumphant Christ, but the suffering Christ on the cross. In this search and reorientation Suzanne was to become a guide and prophet for many.

Women witness in the Latin quarter

When at the end of August 1914 Suzanne came to Paris she had no clearly defined job, nor for some time any access to private funds. There was some understanding that she would work among women students from Eastern Europe, but in Paris no foyer as yet existed which could serve as a basis for such work. Allier of the Fédé did not really know what to do with this "German" lady from Alsace, and Suzanne had much more empathy with the student volunteers than with the president of the Fédé.

With no clear work assignment, Suzanne once again attempted to do far too many things at the same time. She developed contacts with foreign women students who were cut off from their countries because of the war. She followed courses at the institute for social studies and occasionally had Greek lessons. She started several discussion groups in the SCM and at the YWCA. She also explored the Latin quarter where thousands of foreign students lived in miserable conditions; she herself changed lodgings five times during the early years of the war. Proudly she wrote to Marguerite Ecoffey: "With my saints, my books, my table constantly cluttered with papers, letters and brochures, a Russian recently told me that my study had the same atmosphere as that of an authentic student 'intellectual proletariat'. You can imagine how flattered I was and how I like this much more than our bourgeois lounge in Lausanne."

Gradually Suzanne's life received a clearer direction. This was to a large extent due to "the great Suzanne", a remarkable French woman who is too little known although she played an important role in ecumenical history: Suzanne Bidgrain. Born in 1879 in a highly cultured, agnostic family of Normandy, she had a great gift for languages, a typical French Cartesian mind, a strong will and a compassionate heart. She read the

Bible for the first time when she was twenty-five. Abhorring all superficial knowledge, she decided to examine the sources of the faith which she accepted, and went to study theology in Marburg where in 1912 she founded the first women's branch of the German SCM. She continued her studies in Glasgow and in 1915 graduated with a master of arts with honours. Meanwhile she had met Ruth Rouse who awoke in her a great interest in the ecumenical movement. It was the WSCF which made possible her appointment as travelling secretary for the women's branch of the Fédé from 1916 onwards. So the "little" and the "great" Suzanne — as they called each other — met. They became friends and their often very intimate correspondence covers the period from 1918 to the late 1950s.

The "great" Suzanne's way of working was to stay for several months in a French university town to form the solid nucleus of an SCM women's group, and then move on to another university centre. Meanwhile the "little" Suzanne got more and more deeply involved in the Latin quarter of Paris through various study circles on social and missionary questions and Bible study groups. Both Suzannes were keen to reach beyond the limited group of French Protestant students and to come into contact with Orthodox and Roman Catholic Christians as well as with seekers and agnostics, learning from them and witnessing to them. "To our small women's association in Paris we invited priests and people of all kinds...," recalled the 80-year old Suzanne. "I remember a student who did not come from a Protestant background at all telling me: 'The only place in the Latin quarter where one can talk about everything is the Fédé.'"[4] This was the Fédé of the women students who, from 1917, had their own centre in the rue Jean de Beauvais, only a few steps from the Sorbonne, called *Entre nous* ("among ourselves"); it also functioned as a foyer so that finally there was a base for the work among foreign women students in Paris.

Not far from this women's centre, from 1917 onwards, the Russian SCM in exile met. After the war their premises in the rue Dupuytren became the meeting place for an early ecumenical study circle attended by a remarkable group of people. Among them were the Orthodox Leon Zander, secretary of the Russian SCM in exile, the philosopher Nicolas Berdyaev, and Paul Evdokimov, a young Russian immigrant who became one of Suzanne's closest friends. Catholics were represented by Father Laberthonnière of the religious order of the Oratorians, Father Gillet who became the general of the Dominicans, and the philosopher Jacques Maritain. Among the Protestants were pastors Marc Boegner and Wilfred

Monod. The "little" Suzanne received her basic ecumenical training there.[5]

The work developing among women students had the strong support of Henri Bois, professor at the theological faculty in Montauban. From 1916 he put at their disposal a house at Mâlons in the Cevennes area of France. For women SCMers this became as much a "holy place" as Domino had been — and became once again after the war — for the male students of the Fédé. In the summer camps at Mâlons Bois was always the main speaker, and Suzanne often led the Bible studies, basing them for the first two years on Paul's Letter to the Philippians and on the beatitudes.

Through financial help from the USA, the women's branch of the Fédé was able to buy a building in the boulevard Saint Michel, the very centre of the Latin quarter, and develop it as an international women's student hostel and meeting place. An American YWCA worker, Sarah Watson, was appointed director, but the work was carried on under the auspices of the French SCM. Suzanne was asked to make sure that the atmosphere in the house and the work itself did not become too Anglo-Saxon but reflected something of the spirit of the Fédé.

The anguish of the post-war period

Throughout the war Suzanne remained uncertain about the best way to live her commitment as a volunteer for Christ. Until 1918, when she officially became the secretary of the women's branch of the Paris SCM, she had no official function (and no salary during her whole SCM period in France). For a short time she was involved in popular education with a group of factory girls in a Paris centre belonging to the popular mission. She spent two summers in Saint Véran, an isolated village in the French alps, where her fellow volunteer, Gourhan, had become a deaconess-evangelist. There she preached for the first time in her life. But work in the proletarian or the peasant milieu did not really satisfy her. She was aware that her gifts lay primarily in the field of leadership training in the student world. But with no official assignment and no further support from the SCM chairman, she could not fully test her vocation. Only when Bidgrain arrived on the scene was she able to do so and to be confirmed in it. That vocation led to a worldwide involvement, especially in the fields of Bible study, ecumenical work and prophetic service.

On the day of the armistice, 11 November 1918, the "little" Suzanne wrote to the "great" one: "It is easier to be great in defeat than in victory."

A few days later the same premonition was expressed more vividly in another letter: "With its joyful and noisy crowds Paris gives me the impression of dancing on corpses and ruins. I do not know why there is so much anguish in my heart." In fact, the following three years were a sad time in her life, with long periods of illness and various frustrations. Not that there was nothing to bring her joy. After almost half a century Alsace had again become a part of France. In December 1918 Suzanne visited Reichshoffen and helped to start an SCM group in Strasbourg. The first post-war congress of the Fédé in Montpellier in 1920 brought changes in leadership which provided more space and support for Suzanne's special vocation. From 1922 onwards she was much more involved in the high-school branch of the Fédé, which gave her great satisfaction. Nevertheless, Suzanne felt that she and her generation did not live up to the great aspirations for which Monod, Grauss, de Faye and so many others had lived and died. As early as December 1916 she had written to Breitenstein: "I feel with growing bitterness that the peace congress will be dominated by economic considerations and once again will mean only a division of the spoils, nothing more; this is not what our soldiers are fighting for... I fear the 'afterwards' more than the present."[6] No wonder many decisions of the treaty of Versailles in June 1919 disappointed her.

Sustaining friendships

Except to her friend Marguerite Ecoffey and a few others, Suzanne wrote little about what it meant for her to be a single woman approaching her thirties. Nor does the more intimate journal which she kept from holy week 1916 on and off during her life reveal much about her personal feelings and desires. There is little doubt that she longed for a deep love relationship. She was convinced that "sooner or later celibacy becomes a suffering for a woman" and that it is not good for a man — she added "even less for a woman" — to be alone. Two of her sisters who had physical infirmities similar to her own were married and had children. It was not the bodily disability that made marriage impossible. Nor did the commitment as a volunteer for Christ necessarily include a vow of celibacy. Suzanne greatly rejoiced when her friends fell in love; often she actually helped them to get married. She loved children. Men, young and old, were attracted by her charm and her intelligence. Did she never think of marrying?

There are a few indications that during the years of testing her vocation this was a real issue for her. Commenting on the happy marriage of two of her friends she wrote in 1917: "Even when I see such perfect happiness, it is strange that I want less and less to get married. I feel that my life is mapped out before me and I love it without desire or regret." But she was not always so serene or resigned. When in 1920 the man who could have become the husband of her friend from Lausanne died, Suzanne wrote to her: "Despite everything, it is a privilege to have met once in your life the one person you felt you were made for. This has never happened to me and I am less a woman than others, less complete and less understanding because of it." The question of men-women relationships, especially the complementarity between the two, remained an existential one for Suzanne. In 1922 she wrote again to Ecoffey: "What I miss much more than a husband is a father or a brother... What helps me above all is that in the spiritual realm I have found at each stage men on whose thought and friendship I could lean. I believe that even in the intellectual realm men and women complement and need one another; our intuitions impregnate their thought, they construct with the material our imagination and our sensitivity give them. I always enjoy a conversation with a male student more than with a woman student (unless he is stupid). But I particularly like talking with more mature men. I think if I had married it would have been with a man twenty years older. I would have sought in him stability, life experience, counsel, guidance." [7]

This type of man-woman relationship indeed became the pattern that sustained Suzanne as she lived her vocation in an ever more expanding ministry. Jules Breitenstein, Charles Grauss and Henri Bois had been fatherly friends and counsellors. Now Marc Boegner began to fulfill this role. He was her pastor in the parish of Passy. In 1920 he was vice-chairman, and from 1923 to 1939 chairman, of the Fédé, with Suzanne as one of the vice-chairpersons for the same period. There were other such sustaining friendships — with Pierre Maury and Paul Evdokimov, later with Willem A. Visser 't Hooft, Théo Preiss, Robert C. Mackie and Hendrik Kraemer. All these men were married. In order to avoid any ambiguity Suzanne always attempted to build a good relationship with their wives. In her friendships with men Suzanne undoubtedly must have felt a restrained sexual attraction, but for her the cause both she and these men served came first.

This inevitably meant that there were moments of great loneliness in her life. Suzanne then turned to God, the one friend whose presence she always sought. Her intimate journals are in fact one long dialogue: most entries consist simply of notes on biblical readings and meditations. She put down in writing what she thought God was telling her. Thus listening to God and meditating on God's word, she also responded in her journals through very intimate written prayers.

NOTES

[1] SdD, "Idéal religieux", *Le semeur*, January 1920, pp.98f.

[2] Rémi Fabre, "Un groupe d'étudiants protestants en 1914-1918", *Mouvement social*, no. 122, 1983, pp.75-101.

[3] Annex to SdD, *Draft Letter* of 13 February 1916 to Raoul Allier.

[4] Chambron, *Interview with SdD*, transcript, pp.9f.

[5] SdD, "Expériences œcuméniques", *Foi et vie*, 1960, pp.179f. and Marc Boegner, *L'exigence œcuménique*, Paris, 1968, pp.36f.

[6] SdD, *Draft Letter* of 31 December 1916 to Breitenstein.

[7] SdD, *Letters* of 20 August 1917, 22 August 1920 and 1 May 1922 to Ecoffey.

5
Expanding Horizons

"I feel as if I've been asked to climb that mountain," said the "great" Suzanne to the "little" one, pointing to the forbidding north wall of the Schreckhorn (literally, the "frightening peak"). It was 1920 and the two were attending a meeting of the World Student Christian Federation at Beatenberg in the Swiss Alps. Bidgrain had been asked to become a travelling secretary for the WSCF, taking over from Ruth Rouse. Suzanne de Diétrich represented the French SCM at the WSCF general committee. For her this was the beginning of more than twenty-five years' involvement with that international student organization. For both Suzannes the Schreckhorn became a symbol of the task ahead — endless travelling, trans-cultural and trans-confessional gatherings, and meeting one deadline after another.

Both of them now learned to see beyond the frontiers of France. They had to look at the 1914-18 war not only through French but also German eyes. And they discovered that, seen through Asian eyes, the so-called first *world* war had only been a European war. World history did not necessarily follow developments in the Western world, and the same events were experienced differently in different continents.

Planning for the future
1895-1920: The WSCF had completed twenty-five years of work among students. There were plans to celebrate this anniversary by holding the general committee in the Swedish castle of Vadstena where the movement had begun. However, the French and German SCMs felt that the post-war situation did not justify celebration. The strong Chinese, Japanese and Indian SCMs were deeply involved in the Asian revolution. They did not want to look backwards but plan ahead for the future. John R. Mott was now 55 years old, and losing contact with the new student generation; the same was true of other officers.

All this meant that important policy decisions had to be taken. Could the WSCF assume responsibility for student relief in post-war Europe?

How could the Federation become more democratic so that students themselves, men *and* women representing different cultures, languages and races, could be better involved in decision-making? From the early years North American, British, some of the continental European, Asian and South African SCMs had participated in the life of the Federation, but now new movements had sprung up in eastern Europe and there was growing interest among students and universities in South America and Africa. How could this expanding constituency be served through WSCF work? The salaries of Mott and partly also of Ruth Rouse had been met from outside sources: how could funds be found for employing a new and larger staff team? What was called for was not a celebration but extensive planning and restructuring.

Mott resigned as general secretary but remained chairman of the Federation until 1928. It was decided that he would be assisted by two vice-chairpersons, one of them a woman. Michi Kawai from Japan was the first woman to hold the post; she was succeeded by Suzanne. The enlarged general committee elected an executive committee of which Suzanne was a member from 1928 to 1935, when she started work as a WSCF secretary. From 1920 to 1925 the central offices were gradually transferred from New York and London to Geneva where the League of Nations had established its office. Languages other than English began to be used at conferences and for publications. The new staff team included, besides Bidgrain, T.C. Koo from China, Margarete Wrong from Canada and Henry-Louis Henriod from Switzerland who led the team. In addition to such internal reorganization, more fundamental issues had to be faced. How was the WSCF to respond to the new world situation? How could it maintain the unity of faith within its fellowship?

The war had transformed the world. Analyzing the new situation Suzanne wrote: "The myth of so-called 'Christian nations' did not survive. The 'prestige' of the West is gone for ever; tribute may be paid to Western science, but no longer to Western civilization. The Chinese renaissance movement is a typical instance of the awakening of anti-Christian feeling and national consciousness in Far Eastern countries. 'Modern thought' has its strongholds now in Japan and China as well as in Chicago or Sydney." [1]

The mood differed from continent to continent. In Asia SCM members enthusiastically participated in the student revolts and in nationalist movements fighting feudalism and colonialism. For example, C.T. Wang, a vice-chairman of the WSCF, had been the leader of the Chinese delegation at the Versailles peace conference in 1919. In North America

the theme was "building up a new world order". In Europe students were
in "a state of psychological fatigue", leading to "an excessive pessimism
as to the possibilities of human effort". [2] Everywhere there was a shift of
interest from purely spiritual to social questions, and a revolt against the
institutions of the past.

At Beatenberg unity was threatened mainly in the realm of faith. "Do
we still believe in the same Christ?" — that question was raised by a
German member of the executive committee. According to Suzanne it led
to one of the most moving and candid discussions in the Federation. "The
dispute turned on the meaning and centrality of the cross. One after
another, committee members rose to tell simply what Christ and his cross
meant in their lives. That evening, before God, the Federation found its
unity once again." It was a unity which held in tension very different
emphases with regard to what Christ and his cross mean for Christian
involvement in this world. "The German delegates emphasized redemption. They took an eschatological view of the world which seemed to
leave no room for human initiative... The Anglo-Saxon position was
completely the opposite. The responsibility of the Christian in international and social affairs was fundamental to their faith." [3] During the
following decades the debate continued over a more "apocalyptic" and a
more "evolutionary" conception of God's kingdom.

Work in post-war Europe

Suzanne never climbed the Schreckhorn, but after Beatenberg her
horizon steadily expanded. Paris and French youth movements remained
her home base, but even there the accent lay on the international and
ecumenical dimensions of the work. In 1919 Rouse had asked her to
devote three months to an international training seminar on social service
for YWCA leaders in Paris. The work with the international women's
student centre and foyer in the Latin quarter took much time, especially
when there was serious financial difficulty, as in the 1920s. Suzanne
confided to a friend that she had to call on a great deal of humour to work
with the energetic Sarah Watson, the American director of the women
students' centre, and that she had to learn the art of diplomacy. In 1921
she was one of the leaders at the first international student summer camp
which the Fédé organized at the Château d'Argeronne in the north of
France. Often Suzanne represented the Fédé at international student
meetings, beginning with the one in Glasgow on "Students in International and Missionary Questions" in January 1921 where she met for the
first time ecumenical leaders such as Swedish Lutheran archbishop

Nathan Söderblom, and the Anglican William Temple who later became the archbishop of Canterbury and a great statesman of the growing ecumenical movement. In Glasgow she also came to know two British SCM secretaries with whom in later years she often worked, Joseph H. Oldham and William Paton, key figures in the areas of ecumenical social and missionary thought.

Germany became especially important in Suzanne's life and work during the 1920s and 1930s. She visited her sister Marie von Türcke in Thuringen and kept contact with her despite Marie's sympathies for the German national front. She helped her financially during the disastrous inflation which in Germany began as early as 1922. Through the von Türckes she came to understand what many Germans thought during the political chaos after the occupation of the Ruhr by French and Belgian troops. Through international student meetings and frequent travel to Germany Suzanne also got to know several German student leaders who resisted national socialism, among them Hanns Lilje, the general secretary of the German SCM, and Reinhold von Thadden, a vice-chairman of the WSCF. Developments in Germany filled Suzanne with growing apprehension. In a circular letter of November 1930 as WSCF vice-chairperson she wrote from Paris: "The European atmosphere has become heavier in the last month than it has ever been during the past twelve years; something of the pre-war nervousness has swept over this country after the German elections... A few months ago, another European war seemed to me unthinkable; but are there limits to human madness?"

Work with east European women students in the foyers of Lausanne, Geneva and Paris had prepared Suzanne well for participation in WSCF meetings in Eastern Europe. Baron Nicolay, a Finnish Lutheran pietist, had started evangelistic Bible study work among students in Russia, and out of it grew the Russian SCM of which Lydia Menzinger, Suzanne's Russian friend, became a member. Rouse and Mott had visited this movement in 1909. Similar student work had developed in Poland, Romania, Bulgaria, Hungary, Serbia and Greece. However, as long as the WSCF followed no clear ecumenical policy it could not really help with work in essentially Orthodox and Roman Catholic regions.

This began to change in 1911, when the WSCF general committee met near Constantinople with the blessing of the ecumenical patriarch, which led to a promising development of SCM work in eastern Europe. As early as 1913 the Russian SCM was accepted as a member of the Federation and a south-east Europe commission was appointed to make a survey of student needs in that area. The 1915 general committee should have met in Prague, but war and the Russian revolution upset all such plans.

At Beatenberg south-eastern Europe got much attention in policy-making, and both Bidgrain and Henriod were to make extensive visits to that area. From 1921 south-eastern European leadership training courses took place annually until 1931, and less regularly up to 1940. Suzanne helped to organize and lead several of these. She was a Bible study leader at the 1922 course at Ceske Kubice in southern Czechoslovakia. In Prague she experienced the tragic situation of the Russian emigrant students; two of them became mentally ill and three committed suicide during her one-week stay in that city.

These eastern European meetings were a hard school of international and ecumenical learning. Both leaders and participants had to cope with great differences in confession and language (the courses often used German, French and Russian), as well as with extreme and often opposing nationalist feelings. In 1930 Suzanne was asked to preside over the course in Truskawiec at the foot of the Carpathian mountains in Poland, and almost thirty years later she still remembered the difficulties she faced: "The group consisted of Orthodox from Romania and Bulgaria, Protestant and Catholic Hungarians, Czechs and Poles. Humanly speaking, there was no ground for meeting, in temperament, strong national feelings, ecclesiastical membership, and theological conceptions. There were crises. There always are if you go beyond superficial friendships, and if ecumenical dialogue is taken seriously. We make one another suffer, because the truth of God is at stake which each one comprehends from a different point of view. The same question [as at the Beatenberg committee] comes back in different ways: Do we serve the same Christ? On that particular occasion certain Orthodox attacked our Protestant individualism and asked for a biblical interpretation based on the church fathers."[4]

Suzanne never had the opportunity to visit Russia, but in Paris she became a link between the Fédé and the Russian SCM in exile. She invited Leon Zander to help with the leadership of the course in Trus-kawiec. She also participated actively in French-Russian retreats which were organized near Paris, such as the one at Boissy in November 1930 where, together with Nicolas Berdyaev, she introduced the subject "The Church and the Ecumenical Question".The most memorable east European travel for Suzanne was to Bulgaria in August 1935 where the WSCF general committee met in an old palace at Chamcoria. She presented the report on ecumenism. It was there that Willem A. Visser 't Hooft, the new general secretary of the Federation, asked her to come and work part-time as his colleague at the Geneva headquarters.

The discovery of North America

The almost frighteningly energetic YWCA worker Sarah Watson of the international student centre in Paris was for Suzanne the symbol of North America. "How I would like to have an American *body!*" Suzanne once wrote to Bidgrain. This limited perception of America changed when in 1925 she finally made the much-postponed visit to her sister Adèle Pfalz-graf in Fairfax, Virginia. She combined it with five months of travelling and learning. Towards the end of her stay Suzanne wrote to Marguerite Ecoffey with her usual frankness: "What a world! My first reactions were almost totally negative. Gradually, however, I have come to like it. In this new country there is a spirit of enterprise and adventure which has great charm. Americans are crassly ignorant, they lack tradition and culture, but then how limited are our own horizons, enclosed in our frontiers, narrow-minded, and with all our prejudices." Suzanne later met Americans with a great deal of knowledge, tradition and culture, and she also learned to be less harsh on Europe. This visit was the first of many — five before the second world war and longer visits after the war.

On her first journey, after a few days in New York and Washington, Suzanne went to the deep South. At a "college for coloured people only" in Talladega, Alabama, she attended a student conference as the only white person among some 75 blacks. The intellectual level of the meeting did not impress her; nor did she care for the educational methods. But Suzanne appreciated the black leaders: "They were men and women of great worth, matured through moral suffering, and more sensitive than the whites." She was shocked by the racial discrimination. From Alabama Suzanne went on to a summer conference for white students in North Carolina, and was struck by the contrast: "The whole comfort of a large mountain hotel, a superb view, delightful coolness, and 400 young and cheerful American women in knickerbockers and with short hair."

After this double immersion in American life Suzanne visited her sister, and there she saw something of the harsh realities of rural America. Adèle remembered Suzanne as a 15-year old girl. Their lives had taken such different directions that it was difficult for them to find common ground or interesting subjects for conversation. Nevertheless, Suzanne stayed several weeks with her lonely sister, ostracized by the de Dietrich family.

During the last part of her journey Suzanne participated in American student YMCA and YWCA conferences and visited Chicago, Toronto and Montreal. The highlight was a five-week Bible study course in Ontario which had an impact on her future biblical work. Suzanne often said that Canada was like a second home to her. The beauty of Canadian nature, particularly that of the Algonquin Park where the Bible study course took place, made a deep impression on her: "I have developed a passion for canoeing. It is quite marvellous to glide on the water, watch the birds and explore the rivers. The sunsets on the lakes were unique, as the water was often polished like a mirror; and the nights were full of stars... The Canadians are healthy and full of fun, they swim like fishes and paddle like Indians — simple, true: they have made me feel ten years younger."[5]

Exposure to Asia

Asia was the continent Suzanne knew least. In 1922 she could have gone to the WSCF meeting in Peking, but she chose instead to go to an east European training seminar. She never visited China, Japan or the countries of South-East Asia. But through her books translated into Asian languages and the work of Asian student leaders influenced by her, she made an impact on Bible study in that continent. Suzanne was well aware of the fact that the centre of world history had shifted. After a discussion with student leaders from all continents she wrote: "Suddenly I see the map with new eyes and you [Europe] appear to me as you really are: a peninsula attached to the immense Asia."

A year after Suzanne wrote that, she had the opportunity to immerse herself in part of the Asian world. Twice she visited the Indian sub-continent, in 1928-29 and 1936-37, travelling by train, bus and bullock-cart. During the first journey she represented, together with the political economist André Philip, the French SCM at the WSCF general committee in Mysore. There T.C. Koo and she were chosen as vice-chairpersons. Suzanne introduced the report of the committee on women's work and was asked to make the farewell speech in honour of John Mott. Federation matters were almost pushed to the background by the impact Asia made on her during the four-month journey. Suzanne described it in published travel notes.[6] With her graphic style she transported young readers from Europe to Bombay and showed them the Indian sub-continent through her eyes. The dignity of Indian stewards on the boat; the flying fish of the Indian ocean; the multicoloured crowds in Bombay; the roads through barren areas and jungles; the meeting with the Maharajah of Mysore, a Hindu philosopher-prince who in his welcome speech exhorted the busy Christians not to neglect silence and meditation; a village in South India; an ashram; a home for 15-20 year old widows in Madras; the ordered chaos of Madurai; the Syrian-Orthodox women of the Malabar coast and a marriage feast there; Christian and Buddhist colleges in Ceylon, the red flowers and blue mountains of that island — these and many other sights, people and situations came alive in Suzanne's notes with a detail which perhaps only a first-time visitor with a great gift of listening and seeing notices.

On her second visit Suzanne started in Ceylon. In Colombo she attended an Asian regional conference of the YWCA and in Kandy the YWCA executive committee of which she was a member from 1933 to 1937. Then she went north to India, visiting and speaking at university colleges in Madras, Allahabad, Lucknow, Agra, Delhi and Lahore. She attended an Indian national Christian council meeting in Nagpur and took part in several Indian women's meetings. She sought contact with Hindu and Muslim leaders in Benares and Delhi. While people, landscapes and everyday life had been at the centre of her attention during her earlier visit, this time Suzanne was especially sensitive to the social and political situation, the independence of India for which Gandhi and Nehru struggled together but with different aspirations for the future of the nation. She keenly followed the discussions among Christians, Hindus and Muslims on the mass movements of conversion of low-caste people to the Christian community.

Suzanne never pretended to understand Asian thought and life. Nevertheless, when Europeans and North Americans were annoyed by the incomprehensible sensitivities or awkward silences of Asians, Suzanne became the advocate for her Asian colleagues. Because she could listen with sympathy, she commanded a certain authority in that role. One particular two-day WSCF gathering illustrates this trust friends had in her wisdom with regard to Asian affairs. Without any declaration of war Japan had invaded China in 1932. By 1937 the tension between the two countries was such that even within the WSCF fellowship it seemed impossible for Chinese and Japanese to listen to each other and to plan together. That year Soichi Saito from the Japanese student YMCA had come to the USA as a member of an official Japanese delegation, and T.C. Koo from China was on a lecture tour in America. Francis Miller, then chairman of the Federation, decided to call a meeting in a private home in Virginia to consult together with Koo and Saito about WSCF policy in the Far East. Suzanne happened to be in North America and

Miller invited her to participate in that delicate encounter. She was even asked to introduce the conversations. Despite radically opposed political positions a common Christian faith allowed for corporate planning, and a true mutual understanding was reached. For Suzanne these days were "one of the very great experiences of my life in the Federation", as she wrote to Visser 't Hooft.

A love for South America

Suzanne had a very special love for South America. The call of Charles Grauss in 1913 for dedicated French volunteers to help Latin America was never really forgotten. Only in 1937 could Suzanne herself respond to that call. She had a double mission: as a YWCA executive committee member she was to represent the world movement at the first South American continental YWCA meeting at Piriapolis in Uruguay and visit all YWCA centres in the continent; as a staff member of the WSCF she was asked to make "a survey of the field" by visiting Christian student groups and establishing contacts with various university centres. During this four-month journey she spent a good deal of time in Argentina but she also went to Uruguay, Bolivia, Brazil and Chile. The flight from Buenos Aires over the Cordilleras to Santiago was her very first plane journey. This time too she kept a travel journal in which she vividly described her first impressions as the ship sailed into Rio de Janeiro and then proceeded south to the River Plate and the "geometric city" of Buenos Aires. The insights gained during her visit — some of them quite new at that time and many still relevant today — were communicated to the two world bodies in confidential reports with suggestions for action. [7]

Coming from a Latin culture Suzanne had naively expected to feel at home. Her old friends from the winter of studies in Geneva, Emmanuel and Yvonne Galland, who now worked in the River Plate area, tried to interpret the continent for her. However, she soon stopped speaking about South America as a whole, and its "Latin" character became problematic. The Spanish-Portuguese Latin culture and the impact of the Roman Catholic Church had undoubtedly marked the whole continent with common features, but Suzanne saw that diverse and new types of nations and populations were growing up. Geographically, racially and culturally the River Plate was quite different from Bolivia on the high plateau, and from Chile on the narrow west coast, and Brazil proved to be a world in itself. Different policies for youth and student work were needed for such diverse regions. Moreover, besides Latin influences Suzanne observed a growing North American impact through cinema, commerce and Protestant schools. While she could speak French with the Catholic intelligentsia of the River Plate and in Brazil, far more often she had to communicate in English.

University life on a European pattern was almost entirely absent. With a few exceptions the main faculties of law, medecine and engineering aimed at technical know-how more than knowledge and culture. Moreover, they worked in isolation. One of Suzanne's recommendations was therefore that high-school students should be given priority. She noted that YMCA, YWCA and student work was limited to social service activities and sports, and hardly any spiritual nurture was provided. Most members were nominal Roman Catholics and an explicitly Christian-emphasis programme was considered as proselytizing. Yet during conversations with students in different university centres Suzanne had felt something of the spiritual vacuum in which many lived, and she met a number of seekers. Spiritual help had to be provided. But where could leaders be found for such biblical nurture? Practising Catholics were either already involved in Catholic student work or, if they occupied leadership positions in the YMCA/YWCA, they did so because they considered these movements simply as social service agencies. Suzanne was therefore increasingly interested in the predominantly conservative Protestant church youth groups. Everywhere she sought — and usually made — good contacts with them and she was impressed with the fervour of their faith. In Brazil she even discovered a small student volunteer movement whose members did both evangelistic and social service work.

Suzanne had come to South America with doubts about the legitimacy of Protestant mission. She disliked confessional proselytism. However, she saw the state of a Catholic church which had never had to face the challenge of the Reformation. She discovered a great spiritual thirst and met genuine and liberating Christian faith among Protestants, especially in Brazil and among Indians in Bolivia. Her doubts about Protestant missions vanished. She came to the conclusion "that it is among these evangelical groups that we might find the convinced leadership which would be able to start study groups among students on a limited but solid Christian foundation".

Suzanne herself began to help with leadership training, and her programme became increasingly popular. Almost every day new meetings had to be added for talks, Bible studies and answering questions. The love she felt for South America became mutual. "She has conquered everybody," wrote Emmanuel Galland to Marc Boegner at the end of her stay, and asked for a series of similar visits.

Suzanne's most lasting service was the retreat during passion week 1937 which she led in the home of the Gallands and in which Christian leaders from several countries took part. For this retreat she wrote her well-known meditations on the cross which became her first Spanish publication: *La Cruz* (Buenos Aires, 1937).

Only in 1959 could Suzanne go back to her beloved continent, but her heart was there all the time, and she made sure that South America remained on the ecumenical map.

NOTES

[1] SdD, "A Tentative History of the Federation Message", *The Student World*, 1931, p.113.
[2] SdD, report on "Evangelization", *The Student World*, 1926, p.179.
[3] SdD, *Fifty Years of History*, Geneva, 1994, p.46 (= shortened English ed. of SdD's history of the WSCF, *Cinquante ans d'histoire*, Paris, 1948).
[4] SdD, "Expériences œcuméniques", *Foi et vie*, 1960, p.181.
[5] SdD, letter of 18 September 1925 to Ecoffey.
[6] SdD, "Notes et souvenirs", *Le semeur*, May 1929, pp.475-500; and SdD, "L'Inde à la croisée des chemins", *Le semeur*, June 1937, pp.525-40.
[7] SdD, "Impressions d'Amérique du Sud", *Le semeur*, November 1936, pp.13-25, and her reports to the World YWCA and the WSCF.

Right: the extended family. Seated first left is Suzanne's father, Charles de Dietrich. Fifth from the right is her mother, Anna de Dietrich-von Türcke. Her sisters Adèle and Marie are third and eleventh from the left. Suzanne herself is seated at the front with a cousin (Association amis de Dietrich).

Suzanne with Louise Boillot, ca. 1900 (Fonds SdD).

Charles and Anna de Dietrich on the steps of the "Moulin" with their daughters (from left to right) Adèle, Suzanne, Marguerite and Amélie, end 1890s (Association amis de Dietrich).

The four directors of the de Dietrich company in 1892. Left to right: Albert de Dietrich, Edouard de Turckheim, Eugène de Dietrich (later, Suzanne's guardian), and Suzanne's father (Administration de Dietrich).

Left to right: Marc Boegner, pastor and friend, the Russian Orthodox philosopher Nicolas Berdyaev, and Father Brillais, superior of the Roman Catholic order of the Oratorians, representing the three major Christian confessions at Mouterhouse, 1932 (Fonds SdD).

Karl Barth, centre, whose theology influenced Suzanne mainly through her two friends, Pierre Maury, left, and Willem A. Visser 't Hooft, 1939 (WSCF).

Suzanne with Paul Evdokimov, about 1950 (Photo Fonds SdD).

The WSCF leadership team just after the second world war: Left to right: Philippe Maury, Suzanne, W.A. Visser 't Hooft, John R. Mott, Pierre Maury, Robert C. Mackie, T. C. Koo and Margarete Wrong.

6
The Word for the World

"Suzanne de Diétrich is, as no one else is, 'biblical renewal' in person. Nobody has summed up the harvest of this [biblical] work so fully and clearly. She understands how to present consensus, perhaps precisely because she is not a theologian and therefore does not attempt to produce original thoughts of her own. But she excels in systematically expounding and clearly formulating the theological insights of the Federation — and putting it in poetic language as she did in *L'heure de l'offrande* [her book of meditations on the gospels]."[1]

This is the conviction reached by Hans Mayr after a thorough examination of theological developments in the World Student Christian Federation, giving special attention to the role played by the Bible in the search for Christian "unity and message". How was Suzanne prepared for playing such a role? Did her first and only visit to Palestine in early 1929, on her way back from the Indian sub-continent, contribute to this?

The land of the Bible

"I was apprehensive about Jerusalem and I was wrong. It is a fascinating city in itself, like every oriental city. But it is particularly fascinating for its historical significance." Those who leave disappointed are the people who come with dreams of an ideal Jerusalem, looking for an atmosphere of piety and places and scenes that call for veneration. "Jerusalem is not this at all. Its tragic flavour comes precisely from not being this, but from remaining centred in humanity: both holy and profane, a place of prayer and a converging point of rivalries and hatreds; Jerusalem is the most poignant exemplification of human history under the skies, at once comedy and tragedy... In Jerusalem, more than anywhere else, You remain the eternally crucified, crucified by our ignorance and our pride."[2]

Suzanne's travel notes often turn into a dialogue with Christ. She admired the mosque of Omar on the temple mountain. With pain she saw how in the holy sepulchre Christians tear up the seamless robe of Christ and quarrel over the torn pieces while a Muslim looks on ironically. At the wailing wall she heard an Arab guide: "We allow the Jews to come to weep." She felt close to Mary singing the Magnificat not in Bethlehem, but at Aïn-Karin in the rough Judean countryside. From the shores of the Dead Sea she looked up at Palestine and exclaimed: "How rough and naked is Your promised land!" In Galilee she had hoped to find traces of Christ but found only signs of judgment. "Galilee is dead. And You, You are where there is Life. A soul or a region which knew You and abandoned You can never be more than a desert."

This visit to the land of the Bible and the way Suzanne wrote about it are typical of her relationship with the Bible itself. She went to Palestine and to the scriptures with much expectation, but also with the readiness to let her faith and hopes be challenged and corrected. She never became "biblio-latrous", worshipping the holy book. Intellectual honesty would not allow her to escape critical questions addressed to her or to the biblical text. She knew that God's life-giving word became incarnate in a living person, not in a book, and even less in any footprints of Christ impressed on the rocks of Palestine.

Suzanne looked at the world with eyes enlightened by the incarnate Word. She studied and meditated on the Bible with a mind sharpened by the observation of what really happened in the world. That was how her travel journal could become an inner dialogue with Christ. Her Bible studies and biblical writings have an earthly character, still marked by an engineer's perception of things. At the same time they have a transcendental quality because God's reality breaks in on our human realities, judging them and renewing them. Old Testament prophets strongly influenced this double movement from the word to the world and from the world to the word.

The voice of the prophets

The haloed Christ of the stained-glass window in the church of Niederbronn had been the first to speak to the child Suzanne. Then Jesus on the cross challenged the student who began to study the gospels and the letters of Paul. At first she did not know what to do with the Old Testament, and her biblical guides, Jules Breitenstein and Renée Warnery, could not help her much. In the summer of 1916 she began to explore this unknown territory on her own. Having decided to lead a study group on the prophets, she went away for two months of solitary reading and reflection, as she had done two years earlier in Sweden.

The world situation was critical. Several of her friends were fighting near Verdun in the bloodiest battle of the war, a setting not inappropriate for the study of the prophets. Many years later Suzanne recalled: "For up to eight hours a day I was deep in the study of the Old Testament. In order to speak about the prophets they must first become living persons for us. We must meet them in their own time. The word of God is a *concrete* word, addressed to *concrete* people. It is the living God who acts in history and reveals his secret will to his servants, the prophets. Here are men who do not let themselves be blinded by the passions of the moment, men who dare to go against the current of public opinion, men enabled to discern in daily events God's judgments, God's call and saving purposes. How vital the Bible is in times of war!"[3]

To find her way through the great variety of Old Testament books Suzanne took along the *Introduction to the Old Testament* by Lucien Gautier, professor at Geneva. When she had finished her study outlines, she sent them to both Breitenstein and Gautier for criticism. The first was "full of admiration for the tremendous work and great erudition", but as a New Testament teacher he did not feel qualified to offer criticism. But he added: "It is a pity that you do not know Greek and Hebrew as the women humanists did. You would be a real theological force and you could help to set free our exegesis and biblical theology from dependence on Germany." Impressed by the competence and enthusiasm with which Suzanne had entered the world of the Hebrew prophets, the much older Gautier wondered whether he should not now address her as "colleague". He addressed her as "my dear friend", because "the friends of my friends, the prophets, are my friends". He advised her on further reading and said that in a few months he could teach her enough Hebrew to read large sections of the Old Testament. As a specialized scholar he expressed amazement that Suzanne had dared to prepare study material on the *whole* Bible, both the Old and New Testament.

Why did Suzanne never take the time to learn Hebrew and to perfect her Greek? She continuously learned from the research of biblical scholars, but she did not want to get caught in esoteric discussions over linguistic, historical and theological details in which scholars often indulge. She wanted to remain among the lay people. With the whole Bible before her, she remained passionately interested in the questions the world asks while listening to the questions and commands God addresses to politicians and teachers, to lawyers and labourers. Such simultaneous listening to the word and the world gave Suzanne a special prophetic discernment. In the tradition of her spiritual ancestors of Ban de la Roche, it led her to prophetic speaking and action. Her first published article on the prophets (1920) shows the empathy she felt, for instance, with the lonely figure of Amos. "'The lion has roared; who will not fear? The Lord Yahweh has spoken; who can but prophesy?' The whole of Amos is present in these two lines: the son of the desert, the prophet of Yahweh. This meditative Oriental, the shepherd from Tekoa, knew how to observe nature and human persons with a particular acuteness. His style, thinking, ethics, faith are indelibly marked by the desert. His philosophy is sombre, like the setting where it was born; his images are sombre, too. He heard the roaring of the hunting lion, the roar of the satisfied animal; the lion does not roar without reason... He heard the trumpet of war which caused alarm in the cities; has this terrible sound ever been heard unless the enemy was approaching?... The voice of the prophet would not be raised unless Yahweh had provoked it. The cities would not be destroyed unless Yahweh had wanted it. The desert has its laws, and history has its."[4]

Suzanne did not remain with the fierce judgments of Amos only. Hosea taught her much about God's incomprehensible love and steadfastness. From Isaiah and Ezekiel she learned something of the awe mediated by the holy presence of God. Jeremiah, the suffering prophet, was close to her heart. The words of the unknown prophet of the Babylonian exile, collected in Isaiah 40-55, comforted her. The prophecies of Haggai and Zechariah gave her courage to renew her hopes when they had been shattered. All these prophets strengthened Suzanne in her social consciousness and her struggle for justice. Their words and acts opened her eyes for a history beyond history.

Biblical apprenticeship

Before 1914 the Fédé organized biblical lectures only. It was Suzanne who began leading Bible studies in camps and study circles of the women's branch of the Fédé and the French YWCA. Reporting at the Fédé congress in 1920, she said: "In every place where Bible study is done in a group (and intelligently, of course), it rapidly becomes one of the essential activities of the Association, one of the reasons for its existence."[5] In that report Suzanne for the first time expounded upon her convictions and described her experiences with regard to Bible study.

The *aim* of such a programme of regular Bible study should be fourfold: (1) Bible study groups are important for the growth of fellowship. Confronted with the exigencies of the time and the promises of God, group members often enter into free conversation, sharing intimate experiences and personal doubts which they would hesitate to express elsewhere. Lasting friendships have grown in this way. (2) The best way to share the Christian message with outsiders is to study the original documents *with* them, listening to their objections and entering into their problems. (3) Bible study develops and strengthens faith. For many it has become the starting point and the unfailing resource for a continuing spiritual life. (4) Such studies are a good school for acquiring an understanding of the biblical message, for learning how to approach the Bible and how to let it guide our lives, something Suzanne found almost totally lacking among French students. Here she argued for a historical-critical approach which frees the text from our presuppositions. As in the valley of dry bones the prophetic word of Ezekiel gave flesh to the bones, so knowledge about the original context of biblical passages can give flesh to ancient texts. But only God's breath, which neither historians nor prophets have at their command, can give life to the dead. God's breath can also give life to ancient texts to become God's word for the world of today.

In the same report Suzanne also spoke of the *methods* of doing Bible study. She did not want to prescribe fixed rules. She suggested that study groups should have no more than 12 to 15 persons. For newcomers group reading of biblical passages with only minimal interpretative comments by the leader was a good approach, because the words of Jesus, Paul or the prophets were what was important and should make their own impact. For texts which needed background information one or several group members might be asked to prepare and introduce the study, leading to a general discussion. Still better, a study outline could be given out beforehand with questions to help members in their personal preparation; the group could then meet to share and discuss the insights while the leader was careful to see that it was the biblical text which was discussed and not the study outline. Concerning *difficulties* Suzanne mentioned the need to find and train good leaders: persons who would not monopolize the discussion, but let the group members speak; persons who could start a discussion, if needed, and bring it back to the text when it went astray; persons who were prepared to comment on questions raised when no one in the group dared to speak. Finally Suzanne pointed to the need for study material and biblical commentaries written in French and for lay people.

Today these comments about Bible study may sound commonplace, so much have they become part of our practice. But such participatory studies were revolutionary in 1920. Later Suzanne spoke and wrote much more about the "why" and "how" of Bible study, but the main lines of her life-long commitment to it are already present in that early report.

Preparing Bible study outlines became Suzanne's major occupation, so much so that in 1922 she confided to Marguerite Ecoffey: "Intellectually I have become a machine for producing Bible study plans of different kinds." At that time she was busy working on studies on the prophets for high-school students, on the parables of Jesus for the French YWCA, and on Paul for a Paris student group. A normal two- or three-page outline for a single session dealt with the literary and historical context of the passage to be studied, with a series of questions. These helped the users first to read and examine the biblical text before discovering how God is speaking through it to the present generation. A series of such outlines served for group Bible studies during a whole university semester, a summer camp or a retreat. They dealt with an entire biblical book or focused on various aspects of a biblical theme.

Outlines were first tested in a group. After revision, they usually appeared as a series in a student periodical; only after further revision would they be brought out as a booklet. In 1922 Suzanne's studies on the parables had just reached this third stage. Soon after, similar outlines on "The Hearers of Jesus", "The Apostle Paul", "Jesus in Mark's Gospel" and "Some Characters of the Old Testament" were published as separate booklets and used widely. Today we have a wealth of such material which makes the insights gained in biblical research accessible to a wider public and helps seekers and church members to discover God's word to the world. In the 1920s such literature was almost non-existent.

Suzanne also helped with the training of study group leaders. At the first training camp that met near Paris in 1923, participants were introduced to the thought of Jesus in the synoptic gospels and to the thought of Paul. They then had to write a series of study outlines on these subjects with suggestions on how to use them. During that camp a "biblical commission" of the Fédé was appointed to stimulate such biblical work.

Older French people interviewed about Suzanne invariably mention Mouterhouse. In this small village in a lonely valley near Niederbronn stands the house where Suzanne's parents had lived before she was born. Some Fédé camps had already been held in the house of Suzanne's sister, the "Papéterie" in Wolfershoffen. When in 1923 this was no longer available, Suzanne planned a high-school camp in the de Dietrich house at Mouterhouse. While preparing the unused and practically empty building for the campers she wrote: "It is an ideal place for camps, in the middle of a forest. I dream of equipping this house and organizing a succession of camps during the whole summer." The dream was gradually realized. During the first few years the camps were held in primitive

conditions, but in 1928 the house was repaired and for a small rent the
Fédé could use it for meetings and as a holiday centre. For Suzanne
herself Mouterhouse became a home for solitary retreats and intensive
periods of work. There, several generations of French students discovered
the Bible as a challenging message which questioned and guided them in
their lives. A little-known meeting at Mouterhouse in 1932 was to
become a prophetic milestone in ecumenical history.

Biblical renewal
   A one-month "summer school for Bible study", the famous Mount
Hermon conference in 1886, became the main incentive for founding the
World Student Christian Federation in 1895. There John R. Mott received
the vision for his worldwide ministry and there the Student Volunteer
Movement for Foreign Missions began. The WSCF did not have to wait
for a Suzanne de Diétrich to discover the Bible. A survey on Bible study
in the Federation starts with the affirmation: "From the beginning of the
student movement Bible study has occupied a central and fundamental
place. In the early days it was virtually the only activity." [6]
   At Mount Hermon, as at the early Sainte-Croix conferences and in
most SCMs of the time, the Bible was read as a devotional guide,
confirming the readers in their evangelical faith. "Bible study" meant
either prayerful individual reading of selected passages (the "morning
watch") or listening to devotional biblical talks. An exception was the
British SCM. From 1900 on it encouraged that much more participatory
and analytical type of study which Suzanne came to know in the Lausanne
SCM. Three further developments influenced Bible study in the Federation; Suzanne was closely associated with all of them.
   Formerly most SCMs "were made up of the more pious and definitely
religious students", an observer remarked in 1911. "They now embrace
men in all stages of spiritual development, professing a variety of beliefs,
and shading off into varying stages of doubt and perplexity concerning
Christian faith. Also the Christian student of today is less inclined to try
and keep his faith unrelated to his general knowledge than his predecessor
of ten or twenty years ago." During the war Suzanne's friends at the front
and she herself in her work in the Latin quarter of Paris had felt this
change of mood. With the post-war shift from devotional and evangelistic
concerns to social and international questions, the former ways of
approaching scripture were no longer suitable. This led in 1922 to the first
WSCF consultation on Bible study where leaders involved in this work
gathered at Harderbroek in the Netherlands to exchange experiences and

plan for the future. Suzanne represented the Fédé at this meeting and took an active part in the discussions. It soon became clear that the new situation called for a very earthly, intellectually honest and open kind of study, the approach which Suzanne had already learned to practise. Both in WSCF meetings and in most national SCMs mainly New Testament texts were being studied because it was felt that "for our purpose the New Testament is enormously more important than the Old". [7] Suzanne, and a few others, disagreed. In the new world situation the prophets and the whole Old Testament had spoken strongly to them. "Hosea and Jeremiah have for the moment supplanted St Paul in my heart," Suzanne had confided to Breitenstein as early as 1916.

A second development began when, at its Constantinople meeting in 1911, the WSCF adopted a clear ecumenical policy, opening full SCM membership to practising Orthodox and Roman Catholic believers. This introduced into the fellowship a great variety of spiritualities and theologies, including different understandings of the authority of the Bible and the ways to interpret it. Also the criticism of the church, prevalent among Protestant students in the 1920s, was now being challenged. Suzanne's work with Orthodox and Catholics in the Latin quarter and in eastern Europe, her collaboration with the Russian SCM in exile, and her friendships with ecumenically open people like Marc Boegner and Paul Evdokimov prepared her for pioneering in the field of interconfessional Bible study.

The third development was linked with the growing disillusionment about world peace, the impact of the great economic crisis of 1929 and the subsequent rise of dictatorships. In Europe this led to a new type of theology: a biblically based teaching about God, the human predicament and world history, which was critical of the naive belief in human progress inherited from the Age of Enlightenment. The key for understanding, judging and redeeming all things was the death and resurrection of Jesus Christ. Karl Barth, a Swiss systematic theologian who taught in German universities, became its main exponent. In 1926 Suzanne had said in a report on evangelization that in order to respond to the needs of the time the Federation had to bring students much more than a philosophical system or a simple message of international and social brotherhood. "It must bring Christ himself in his creative fullness — not partial solutions, but a new point of view from whence all things will appear in a new perspective." [8]

Many found this new perspective in Barth's theology. It strongly influenced the struggle of those Christians in Germany who formed the

Confessing Church which fought against Hitler's glorification of the Aryan race and his claim that the national socialist state had absolute authority. The biblical renewal movement which started in the WSCF was also influenced by this new theology, though it should not be identified with it. Besides Barth and the American theologian Reinhold Niebuhr, outstanding exegetes played a prominent role, for instance Gerhard von Rad and Julius Schniewind from Germany, Edwyn Hoskyns and C.H. Dodd among Anglo-Saxons, and Wilhelm Vischer and Oscar Cullmann in Switzerland and later in France. Members of the British SCM jokingly coined a new version of the great commandment: "Thou shalt love the Lord thy Dodd and thy Niebuhr as thyself." Suzanne's significant involvement in these developments made her an ideal interpreter of what was happening theologically in Europe. No wonder that in 1937 the World YWCA asked her to do such interpretative work in the USA.

These three developments put the whole Bible at the centre of the life of the WSCF. Biblical articles appeared frequently in the WSCF journal *The Student World*. A three-week Federation seminar, planned for 1934 and to be devoted exclusively to Bible study, was to take place in Mouterhouse but lack of funds made this impossible. Instead, a symposium on "The Bible as Meeting Place" was published. The seminar planned for 1934 finally took place in 1937 at Bièvres, the new conference centre of the Fédé near Paris. It surpassed all expectations. Participants did not take for granted that they already knew the Bible. Suzanne often quoted Visser 't Hooft's description of that seminar: "[We] worked hard for a new understanding of the Bible as a whole for our life as a whole... The Bible becomes silent when we try to force it to answer our questions. It speaks when we come to it as seekers for the truth of God. The alternative is not whether we read the Bible 'piously' or 'historically' or 'critically', but whether we read it egocentrically or theocentrically." [9] Out of the Bièvres seminar came the booklet *Ten Studies in the Gospels* to which Suzanne contributed, and at Bièvres also the first advisory committee met to discuss a WSCF book on Bible study methods.

What was the new understanding of the Bible gained through the biblical renewal movement? The life and excitement are lost if we try to summarize it. Something of what happened can be learned by reading one of Pierre Maury's fictional dialogues where he reconstructs how in an ecumenical Bible study group people from different continents and confessions attempt to learn together what the biblical message teaches them. [10] Looking back at what had happened in the 1930s, Suzanne described in 1955 the gist of the biblical renewal as follows: "A theological revolution swept over Europe which was soon to mark deeply the life of the Federation. Barth and Brunner were its early sponsors; the Confessing Church in Germany became a living embodiment of this theological renewal, often called neo-orthodoxy. The word of God was again proclaimed as a living power, the power by which the church lives. Then the rediscovery of the word led to a rediscovery of the church. Neo-orthodoxy cuts across old categories of fundamentalism and liberalism. The written word is only the medium through which God speaks his living word to us here and now; but it is the necessary medium, chosen by God for this purpose. The whole Bible tells about the redeeming activity of God, and its centre is the incarnation, death and resurrection of Jesus Christ. The parts must be interpreted in the light of the whole, starting from the centre, which is God in Christ."[11]

Biblical mentors

Nobody reads and understands the Bible without being consciously or unconsciously influenced by others. Suzanne's great biblical mentor, Jules Breitenstein, could no longer fulfil that role. He suffered from acute attacks of rheumatism. In 1930 he became totally paralyzed, and after much suffering he died in 1935. Who were Suzanne's mentors in the late 1920s and the 1930s? Four persons would be astonished to find themselves mentioned together: a non-confessional American engineer, a German-Swiss systematic theologian, the French Roman Catholic founder of a religious order at the time of the counter-Reformation, and a Russian Orthodox writer and mystic.

The first was Henry B. Sharman, an engineer from California who had made a fortune by inventing and producing a special type of cover for manholes. With it he bought the wilderness camp Minnesing in Algonquin Park in Ontario, Canada, for running annual Bible study camps. Here he helped generations of North American students and youth leaders to discover the Jesus of the gospels and passed on to them his passion for this Jesus. Twice Suzanne spent several weeks at the Sharman seminars, the first time during her visit to North America in 1925. Both the man and his teaching impressed her deeply. "If only I had met him earlier! My work would have been so different," she confided to Marguerite Ecoffey. "Coming into contact again with the historical person of Jesus has fully cured me of my inclinations towards Catholicism. It has brought out my basic individualism and independence again, and it has cleared up a number of uncertainties and doubts."

Suzanne made plans to invite Sharman to Europe, and translated some of his studies. "He had no use for the church," she recalled in 1955. "He hated ready-made theological affirmations. He wanted us to study the gospels with an 'unprejudiced mind', as though for the first time. Our sole textbook was a synopsis of the three gospels prepared by him, *Records of the Life of Jesus*. He used the Socratic method, proceeding by questions." The campers had to examine carefully the different versions of a saying of Jesus and were challenged to discover for themselves the meaning of the passage and to arrive at a truth and faith which would really be their own. "Sharman's strong personality marked the group so that most of us finally came to the same conclusions — his own. His passionate search for truth, his love for and commitment to the person of Jesus are unforgettable." Thirty to forty men and women went each summer for six weeks to the wilds of Canada to study the gospels for three hours a day. They could hear the cry of the diving birds, wild bears came to their very door, they went canoeing and explored lakes and rivers. "The same spirit of adventure seemed to govern both our theological search and our outings. We experienced freedom in mind and body. And such freedom is a rare thing." [12] This was not written in the spur of enthusiasm but much later, in 1955. Suzanne had by then a biblical theological approach quite different from that of Sharman. She nevertheless felt very grateful to him and kept in touch with him.

A second mentor was Karl Barth. In 1919 he published his commentary on Paul's letter to the Romans which, in its revised edition of 1922, became the seminal document for the radical new theology. At that time Suzanne still worked with the highly analytical historical commentaries of Johannes Weiss and Adolf Deissmann. There is no indication that in the early 1920s she read Barth. From friends in Germany and at the WSCF in Geneva she had heard about him, and she admired his prophetic stand against Hitler. But what she knew of his polemical and radical systematic theological writing did not appeal to her. Perhaps it sounded too "German". Only when Barth lectured in Paris in 1934 could she meet him. Almost reluctantly she wrote to Visser 't Hooft: "Finally I was more in agreement with Barth than I had expected." A few months later she worked together with this controversal theologian at the WSCF summer conference at La Châtaigneraie, near Geneva. What impressed her was his radical theocentric way of thinking and his *theological* interpretation of the Bible. Much of what Suzanne herself had discovered through study and suffering she found confirmed, and deepened, by his writing and preaching. She appreciated in particular the theological biblical commentaries of Barth and other exegetes influenced by him.

It is significant that the main impact of Barthian teaching on Suzanne came through Visser 't Hooft, and even more so through Pierre Maury who had been general secretary of the Fédé and who worked from 1930 to 1934 for the WSCF. This Mediterranean friend of her second mentor she once described as follows: "A Barthian? That he certainly is, but 'à la française'; in other words, with a certain inward liberty and independence. He is a Barthian, while at the same time remaining himself. And through him, the theological and biblical renewal became for a whole generation of young French pastors, SCM members and parishioners a living and lived reality. Doctrinaire he is, but this man — who preaches both absolute corruption and absolute grace — has a marvellous delight in everything human. Art, literature, detective stories — nothing is foreign to him. And then there is the friend... always overworked, he can always spare the time to help a friend in trouble, and when he is with you he gives you his whole self, with the faith and heart of a friend and pastor." [13]

With such a Barthian Suzanne felt totally at home, but she had become wary of dogmatism. She never read the whole of Barth's *Church Dogmatics* and she did not like the intellectualist and dogmatic stance of many of his followers. After a long visit to the Italian SCM in 1935 she wrote to Visser 't Hooft: "I must confess that on my journey the most intelligent people I met were always Barthians. But in Italy, as elsewhere, I felt how quickly the young Barthians could fall into a somewhat dry and proud intellectualism." She herself never became a Barthian. Much of what may appear as Barth's influence on Suzanne's teaching came not from him but directly from the Bible. Once she spoke about a painful experience during her youth, and how she suddenly discovered what grace means and how Jesus does not judge as human beings do, and added: "I did not need Barth to discover grace, for I discovered it at that moment."

Her third mentor Suzanne met on a train journey from Amsterdam to Paris in 1929. She travelled in the same compartment with two Oratorians, members of a French Roman Catholic order Pierre de Bérulle (1575-1629) had founded at the time of the counter-Reformation. This religious community of priests and lay brothers endeavoured to reform the Roman Catholic Church from within. The two members of the order introduced Suzanne to Cardinal de Bérulle's thinking and spirituality, and she wrote a few months later: "It was one of those shocks of the Spirit which don't exactly open up a new world as crystallize latent convictions and bring them together in a form we feel instinctively but haven't yet been able to formulate."

What impressed Suzanne in de Bérulle's spirituality was the radical theocentrism which, she immediately added, one finds also in Calvin's theology. True faith is the worship of God with no other motive than adoration of God at all times. It is to worship and love the will of God, whether God speaks to us or remains silent, whether from a human point of view we succeed or fail. None worships God in this true way except Jesus Christ. The mystery of the incarnation is in this sense not primarily our salvation but the fact that through Christ God now has a true worshipper. Our vocation is to enter into intimate communion with Christ in the various stages of his life from the crib to the cross so that we can participate in this true worship. Suzanne saw here what the apostle Paul meant when he taught that our call is to be in Christ and to have Christ in us, and what the Jesus of John's gospel meant when he insisted that we can bear fruit only if we remain in him.

Suzanne was particularly sensitive to the role de Bérulle played in the development of a *French* school of theological thinking and spirituality. She did not yet use the term "indigenous", but this was her concern. Just as many British Christians became "Anglicans", not Roman Catholics or continental European Protestants, so she felt that the church in France should become "Gallican", close to French ways of thinking and feeling. Once she confided to Visser 't Hooft: "If a 'Gallican' church existed, tomorrow I would be a member of it." She was unhappy about the fact that since the nineteenth century French Protestantism had been, intellectually and spiritually, under foreign influence. "What could be less French, in fact, than the [Anglo-Saxon] theology of revival with its highly emotive and subjective character?" She wanted a return to the "great tradition" of French Protestantism, "which is both Catholic and Reformed, in which God is the centre of the universe and we prostrate ourselves completely to God's will". Inspiration could come from outside, but not guidance: French Protestant theological thought needed "the equilibrium of opposites... It is essentially harmonizing... just because it remained, not 'Roman', but 'Catholic' in the richest sense of that term."[14] Suzanne noticed the parallelism between the Bérullian God-centred reaction versus the humanist man-centred thinking of the sixteenth century, and Barth's God-centred reaction against the concentration on the humanist aspirations of the nineteenth. It is difficult to say whether Barth's theology prepared her for the discovery of de Bérulle's spirituality or vice versa.

A fourth major influence on Suzanne's reading of the Bible came from the Orthodox church, particularly through her friendship with Paul Evdokimov. Others had already taught her much about Orthodox theology and spirituality, among them the Russian emigrants Leon Zander, Nicolas Berdyaev and Serge Boulgakov. Yet it was in the home of the Evdokimovs in Menton in the south of France that Suzanne really learned to appreciate the soul of Russian Orthodoxy.

Her relationship with Evdokimov was a complex one. A Russian emigrant who had come to France in 1923, Evdokimov was ten years younger than her, but her friendship with him and his wife Natasha was one of equals. Yet Evdokimov also became a mentor to her, and the two had long spiritual conversations. They explored the meaning of worship as essentially an act of adoration. Suzanne learned about the liturgical symbolism of Orthodox worship which anticipates the future glory. This led to reflection on the cosmic dimensions of redemption and the living of one's faith in anticipation of the coming transfiguration of all.

Through these conversations Suzanne became deeply aware of the reality of the church. She was especially attracted by the Orthodox understanding of tradition and authority, so different from Protestant individualism and Roman Catholic juridical authority. From the Orthodox she learned to think of tradition as "a river whose current carries us. To be in the church means to be carried by this current which has its origins in the earliest Christian centuries. It means to move in it freely." [15] The friendship with the Evdokimovs also confirmed Suzanne in her meditative reading of the Bible. What she had learned already from Tommy Fallot she now saw much more clearly: the prophetic dimension of our vocation must be kept together with the priestly dimension, with prayer and the sacrifice of praise.

L'heure de l'offrande

"Now at the time of the incense offering, the whole assembly of the people was praying outside. Then there appeared to Zechariah an angel of the Lord..." (Luke 1:10f.). From this passage Suzanne took the title of her first major book: *L'heure de l'offrande: Notes en marge de l'Evangile* (Paris, 1935: literally "the hour of the offering"; the English edition is entitled *Behold Thy King: Meditations on the Gospel*, London, 1938). Here it is not the author of the Bible study outlines, Suzanne the teacher, who is speaking, but the Suzanne who prays and meditates, though the two can never be completely separated. She takes readers into the praying assembly in the temple court, to join the crowd in giving praise and waiting for the message of the angel.

Forty-three passages from the synoptic gospels and a concluding text from the Letter to the Hebrews are chosen for the meditations, and they are presented on the first page of each short chapter; thus she gave the biblical text priority over the comments on them. With a few exceptions these comments do not go beyond a few pages. They are written in such concise, poetic prose that they cannot and should not be summarized. This, of all her books, was dearest to her heart. For many thousands of people it has become a bedside meditation volume, and it could remain so for centuries, for it is a classic of Christian spirituality. The book passed through a long process of maturing before it was published. From 1928 Boegner encouraged Suzanne to take time for writing more than study outlines and "to seal in writing your vision of Christ". She was in fact doing exactly this in her private journal. The book consists largely of selected and rewritten pages from her inner dialogue with God in this journal, "simple 'notes' written from day to day", as she says in the dedication, "To my friends". She adds: "This book is yours... Many a page arose out of our exchanges of thought." No names are mentioned, but the four biblical mentors immediately come to one's mind.

L'heure de l'offrande is the fruit of a careful synoptic study of the gospel text. Like Sharman she approaches the biblical text with a passionate love for and commitment to the person of Jesus. Like Barth she sees in Jesus not the great founder of a religion but the living Word of God revealing the key for understanding the whole of creation and history. Like de Bérulle she emphasizes the mystery of the incarnation and the need to participate in the different stages of Jesus's life for learning how to live and worship. Like Evdokimov she reads the gospels in an attitude of adoration. Large parts of the book were in fact written in Menton, and Suzanne herself once commented on the Orthodox flavour of the book. However, *L'heure de l'offrande* transcends theological and confessional boundaries. Except for two passages from Pascal, no extra-biblical authors are quoted. Suzanne herself wrote in her dedication: "I firmly believe that with regard to the truth of the gospel there is one Christian and 'catholic' tradition ('catholic' in the etymological sense of the term) for which no church or confession can claim exclusive owner-ship. Ultimately it is nothing other than the continuity of witness which God renders to himself in the church and human souls. My wish and prayer have been not to write anying which would not conform to it."

NOTES

1 Hans O.A. Mayr, *Einheit und Botschaft: Das ökumenische Prinzip in der Geschichte des Studenten Weltbundes*, unpublished thesis, 2 vols, Tübingen, 1975. Quotation in vol. II, A, p.118.

2 SdD, "En Palestine", *Le semeur*, June 1929, pp.541ff.

3 SdD, "Expériences vécues", undated manuscript for a Latin American journal, apparently never published, end 1950s, p.2.

4 SdD, "Prophètes et faux prophètes", *Le semeur*, November/December 1920, pp.100f.

5 SdD, "Rapport sur les cercles d'études bibliques", *Le semeur*, June/July 1920, pp.350-61.

6 Harrison S. Elliott, "The Present Situation in Bible Study in the Student Movements", *The Student World*, 1922, pp.64-84.

7 R. Lawrence Pelly, "The Purpose of Bible Study in Our Movements", *The Student World*, 1912, p.107.

8 SdD, report on "Evangelization", *The Student World*, 1926, pp.184f.

9 Visser 't Hooft, "Editorial", *The Student World*, 1937, p.352.

10 P. Maury, "An International Dialogue on the Bible", *The Student World*, 1934, pp.148-61.

11 SdD, "The Biblical Foundation", *The Student World*, 1955, p.240.

12 *Ibid.*, pp.239f.

13 SdD, *Fifty Years of History: The World Student Christian Federation 1895-1945*, Geneva, WSCF, 1993, pp.57-58 (transl. of *Cinquante ans d'histoire*, Paris, 1948).

14 SdD, "A la recherche d'une doctrine spirituelle, M. de Bérulle", *Le semeur*, March 1930, pp.257 and 260.

15 SdD, "Expériences œcuméniques", *Foi et vie*, 1960, p.184.

7
A Passion for Wholeness

Are we all preaching the same Christ? Do we all believe in and proclaim the unequivocal importance of Christ's sacrificial death on the cross? These questions came up at Beatenberg in 1920. At that first truly international student meeting Suzanne attended, she was immediately confronted with the narrow and painful path one must take in the search for unity. No wonder in her later writings and recollections she goes back to that hour of truth. Through listening to each other's sincere witness the fellowship which had been in danger was kept alive, and the memorable session ended with the revival hymn "When I survey the wondrous cross on which the Prince of Glory died".

When members of student Christian movements worshipped on Sundays they went to different churches. These churches were indifferent, and even antagonistic, towards one another. When social, political and racial implications of the common Christian faith were discussed, deep divisions surfaced within the WSCF itself. Even within national SCMs such divisions were not uncommon. The British delegates at Beatenberg must have thought of what had happened only the previous year in Cambridge: the Cambridge Inter-Collegiate Christian Union, which in 1893 had been a founding member of the British SCM, questioned whether the SCM was still faithful to its basic commitment. In 1919 a delegation of the CICCU asked the SCM leaders: "Does the SCM see the atoning blood of Jesus Christ as the central point of its message?" A CICCU leader present at that meeting later reported: "The answer was, 'No, not as central, although it is given a place in our teaching.' That answer settled the matter, and we explained to them at once that the atoning blood was so much the heart of our message that we could never join a movement which gave it any lesser importance." [1] That decision led to the establishment of the Inter-Varsity Fellowship which linked the more conservative evangelical student Christian unions. The IVF grew steadily, and since the second world war it has been a competing worldwide movement alongside the WSCF.

Ecumenical impatience and involvement

In 1920 Suzanne herself was involved in a controversy in Paris which threatened to divide the French SCM. Under the leadership of Suzanne Bidgrain and the "little" Suzanne the women's branch of the French Fédé had been active during the 1914-18 war. Not only was Bible study now at the centre of its activities but its various study circles also included, besides Protestants, Catholics, Orthodox and free thinkers as members and speakers. Many Protestant men saw this as a betrayal of the Protestant cause. In Paris two separate groupings already met within the Fédé though they often worked together: the Paris Association of Protestant Students and the ecumenically more open study circles like those of the women's branch. The national Fédé had its headquarters at the women's centre. In early 1920 Suzanne wrote to the "great" Suzanne: "There are a number of people here who are very agitated. We are being heavily criticized and it is the women's Fédé that is being accused." Tension grew in the early twenties when some of the volunteers for Christ wanted this movement to have a clearly Protestant stance, while others wanted it to be ecumenically wide open. Suzanne of course fought for the latter position.

The new general secretary of the Fédé, Pierre Maury, felt that what was needed at that moment in Catholic and secularized France was a clear Protestant testimony. The new chairman, Marc Boegner, had much more sympathy for the ecumenical cause, but was at the same time deeply aware of the Protestant heritage and vocation. Both found it difficult to cope with the radical ecumenical impatience of Suzanne. Boegner later commented: "With her outstanding intelligence, her scientific and biblical education and her radiant spirituality Suzanne de Diétrich commanded wide authority; she argued for open ecumenism which, it seemed to me, was unwise at the time. Pierre Maury, on the other hand, was very cautious. His wisdom and authority won, the crisis was resolved and the Fédé was able to continue its work."[2]

The correspondence between Suzanne and Boegner is revealing with regard to ecumenical developments. It covers the period from 1918 to the late 1940s, but unfortunately only part of it has been preserved (all Suzanne's letters and some of Boegner's from the early 1930s are missing). By 1920 Boegner had published the first volume on the life and work of Tommy Fallot, his uncle. He appreciated the urgency of working for ecumenism, all the more so because he had become a friend of the ecumenically open Catholic philosopher Fr Laberthonnière. Now, as the pastor of the parish of Passy in Paris, Boegner was working on the second volume on Fallot, and he became a leading participant at the ecumenical group gathering at the rue Dupuytren where he met outstanding Catholic and Orthodox thinkers. Among his parishioners in Passy was the impatient Suzanne. There was great mutual respect and a growing friendship between Suzanne and Boegner. The eastern silver cross which Suzanne wore every day of her life was a gift from Boegner and symbolized their spiritual friendship. Suzanne helped with catechetical training at Passy. She never tired of making suggestions and critical comments. She was extremely demanding, often expecting too much of her pastor's time and attention. Once she complained to Marguerite Ecoffey: "I have no really intimate friends here — I mean people to whom I can express what I think — except Marc Boegner who is so busy that I only see him every six weeks." In his prayers Boegner must often have both given thanks for and complained about Suzanne. His letters to her are full of sound advice from the pastor, expressions of sympathy and affection from the friend, and irritation from the overworked man. What makes this correspondence ecumenically important is the fact that the two lived at different levels of the growing ecumenical movement. They thus complemented each other, Boegner checking the ecumenical impatience of Suzanne and Suzanne challenging his ecumenical caution.

Through his earlier work as theological teacher at the college of the Evangelical Missionary Society in Paris, Boegner had since 1912 been in contact with leading members of the continuation committee of the world mission conference in Edinburgh in 1910 (which eventually led to the founding of the International Missionary Council), especially with John R. Mott and J.H. Oldham. He also followed with great interest the growth of the Life and Work and Faith and Order movements and their first two world conferences, Stockholm 1925 and Lausanne 1927. He was a friend of the Swedish archbishop Nathan Söderblom, due to whose personal initiative the Stockholm conference was made possible; Charles Brent, the American Episcopal bishop who presided over the Lausanne conference; and the British ecumenist George A. Bell who later became the first moderator of the central committee of the World Council of Churches. In 1928 Boegner was elected president of the French Protestant Federation which represents Protestant churches in France in their dealings with the state, with other confessions and with world ecumenical bodies. However, it was only in 1934 that he participated for the first time in an international meeting. That was in Fanö, Denmark, where the council of Life and Work met to prepare its next world conference, and had to face the question of growing national socialism in Germany and its relationship with the "German Christians", the people within the German churches who collaborated with Adolf Hitler. Boegner made a deep impression at the meeting, and he was soon recognized as a great ecumenical statesman. He became a member, and later president, of the provisional committee of the WCC (1938-48). He was one of its seven presidents from 1948 to 1954, and over the years he undertook many other ecumenical assignments.

It was through Boegner that Suzanne received much inside information about what great ecumenical statesmen thought and what was being planned in official ecumenism. And it was Suzanne who told him about the pioneering efforts in ecumenical youth work.

The living message

In the late 1920s the WSCF fellowship was threatened in three ways. First there was, as we have seen, the challenge from groups such as the Inter-Varsity Fellowship: had the WSCF remained faithful to its primary raison d'etre? How could continuity with the past be maintained while responding to the call to bear witness in a changed world situation? Second, there was the challenge of the geographically and confessionally expanding fellowship. After Beatenberg, member movements from different continents and races could participate in decision-making, but this was not yet possible for member movements of other confessions. The ecumenical policy adopted at Constantinople in 1911 applied only to individual SCM members, not to member movements. Until 1932, when the Russian SCM outside Russia was accepted, all voting members in WSCF committees had come from a Protestant background. The third and most serious challenge to the WSCF fellowship was the fact that in most SCMs, especially in Europe and North America, enthusiasm for evangelism had declined. There was great uncertainty about what Christian faith meant, as Suzanne had shown in 1926 when she presented her report on the evangelization of university students. There was no longer a clear common message to be communicated.

In response to these inter-related challenges the new officers of the WSCF decided in 1929 to start a little-known but significant experiment of ecumenical thinking leading to action. Unity could be found only by honestly facing the existing divisions and through the common search for truth. Thus the "message study"[3] was started. With her ecumenical impatience and readiness for costly ecumenical labour, Suzanne threw herself wholeheartedly into this new venture.

The three official ecumenical world conferences of the 1920s (Stockholm 1925, Lausanne 1927, and the IMC assembly in Jerusalem 1928) had issued "The Church's Message to the World". The WSCF did not intend to issue a similar statement. Instead, it embarked on "a spiritual pilgrimage", a process of mutual listening and witnessing in the context of some of the major issues of the changed world situation. A small message commission initiated and monitored this ongoing process of exchange. It met three times for study-retreats in 1930 and 1931 and issued three message papers. The first was simply an invitation to join this pilgrimage, indicating its urgency, and listing and commenting on a series of guiding questions. The second was a symposium with the suggestive title "A Traffic of Knowledge", where outstanding thinkers from different continents and confessions stated what they believed to be the Christian message in relation to the following issues: secularism; modern concepts of the human person in psychology and education; divinized notions of "Volk" (the people), race, nation; the church and its witness. The third message paper is "A Call to SCMs". The process thus led not to a dogmatic summary of the Christian faith, but to a call to continue the spiritual pilgrimage of a corporate search for truth, to be involved in the quest for unity, in witness among students and in prophetic service to fellow human beings.

The WSCF found itself obliged to reflect theologically on its history. The first message paper starts by retracing that history, because "in order to determine our message for today we must know something of the Federation's 'spiritual pilgrimage'. Our present situation must be understood in the light of our history, and we cannot afford to neglect the great lessons and testimonies of the pioneers of our movement." Suzanne was asked to expand this and show how the Federation's pilgrimage had led to the message study. Unity means not only a fellowship of faith with Christians from different cultures and confessions in our own time, but also unity with the church of all ages. This is a dimension of the ecumenical movement that is often overlooked. It does not mean simply repeating the message as it was understood at another time and in another place. "Life means growth and struggle; unity, not static, but dynamic; unity, not a fact, but a permanent act of faith, to be believed in and fought and suffered for. Unity in truth, and truth in charity, are hard things to strive for... Our unity lies in God's calling; not in what we are, but in him who called us; not in what we may achieve, but in what he did, does and will do; through our standing together in faith and obedience to him, rests our hope and our security."[4]

Maury, the leading figure of this pilgrimage, and W.A. Visser 't Hooft wrote that the WSCF could have no specific message. It was called only to be true, in a new, contemporary way, to God's eternally given message in Jesus Christ. "The gift we received was the realization that the Federation itself is one of God's messages... because it continually seeks to be more faithful to its apostolic vocation." In his own Barthian way Maury added: "God's message to the Federation struck me forcibly as a great call to be men in the fullest sense,... to live in this 'lost world'... because it is a *saved* world, the world which belongs to the risen Christ." No doubt the whole message study was strongly influenced by both the European/North Atlantic situation and by Barthian theology. Nor did it remain unchallenged. Reporting on the meetings of the message commission, Suzanne wrote about the "passion of God" which led participants to challenge one another. "To hurt and make one another suffer is a form of love among Christians when the same passion for truth inspires the partners." At the heart of this pilgrimage was a prayerful search for God's will, "facing together the truth of the gospel in order to find a common interpretation of it for our time". The message study thus became closely linked with biblical renewal.

The sign of Mouterhouse

The living message stressed the search for unity among Christians, and it called for a new reflection on the church and its different confessional traditions. For Suzanne this was nothing new. Already in 1920-21 in the Latin quarter she had conducted what was perhaps the first French study group on ecumenical questions. Participation in the message study meant for her a renewed emphasis on the church. This is reflected in her review, in the early 1930s, of two influential books about the church by Otto Dibelius and Boegner, and in her own study on Paul's understanding of the church as the body of Christ. [5]

Since its beginning the WSCF had been concerned with Christian unity, but in a largely *un*denominational way, without much reference to the church membership of SCM members. In any case most of them were evangelical Protestants or students from other confessions who had little real contact with their own churches. Gradually an *inter*confessional policy developed, and in 1928 a further step was taken; while reaffirming its interconfessional position, the WSCF resolved to "recognize the existence and approve the formation of confessional groups, and seek to enter into relationship with them". The aim was to encourage ecumenism, not to foster an exclusive confessionalism. It was hoped that "by this means the spiritual riches of a particular confession can be brought into the common life in a different way from that which is attained by individual membership only". But for realizing this not only ecumenical resolutions but prophetic acts and signs were needed.

The ecumenical retreat organized from 3 to 8 August 1932 at the de Dietrich house in the isolated village of Mouterhouse in the Vosges became such a sign. It was an enlarged meeting of the mainly European ecumenical commission which the WSCF had set up and whose joint secretaries were Henry-Louis Henriod and Suzanne. Some 35 people, most of them Reformed-Presbyterians, but also Orthodox, Roman Catholic, Anglican and Lutheran, lived together for five days. Except for two Asians and an American, they were all from the European continent and Great Britain. Their reflection centred on Christ's incarnation and the church. It was a closed meeting, almost a secret one, especially because in 1928 Pope Pius XI had issued the encyclical *Mortalium Animos* which expressly forbade Roman Catholic participation in such gatherings. Perhaps that explains why there is no official record; all that is available are the minutes of a preparatory discussion, a group photograph and an article of 1933 reporting on the work of the ecumenical commission, written by its two secretaries.

Prominent among the Roman Catholic participants were Fr Brillais, the superior of the French order of Oratorians, and the Austrian Benedictine Fr Hildebrand; among the Orthodox, Nicolas Berdyaev, Paul Evdokimov, Stephan Zankov, Leon Zander and Nicolas Zernov; among the Anglicans, Enrichi Kan and Fr Gabriel Hebert; and among the Protestants, Boegner, Henriod, Maury, Francis P. Miller and Visser 't Hooft. Several women were present, among them Elisabeth Behr-Sigel, Claire Jullien and of course Suzanne who wrote: "The ecumenical retreat seemed like a harbinger of future events; there was no publicity or noise; it was perhaps one of those acts of faith whose significance and influence remain hidden from men, but over which the angels rejoice... An attic serves as high chamber, and there a few men and women of different races, languages and confessions kneel together in adoration each morning and evening. An artificial unity? Confusion of thought? Not in the least. We were still painfully conscious of the age-long separation of our churches. We could even say that this was never felt more deeply or more poignantly."[6]

On the Sunday morning the division became indeed painful to all. Augustin Ralla Ram from India wanted to wipe out ten centuries of schism at once and celebrate a common holy communion, and the group had to face this challenge from the younger churches in Asia. But in the end, and predictably, the Roman Catholics went to mass in the Catholic village church, the Orthodox celebrated the liturgy in one specially arranged room and the Anglicans in another. Lutherans and Reformed went to the Protestant village church. It was that painfully divided Sunday which all the participants remembered. "I felt a terrible sadness... and committed myself yet again to bringing together the confessions and to the unity of the church of Jesus Christ," recalled Boegner. The common reflection showed the participants how enriching such a corporate prayerful search for truth can be. Visser 't Hooft wrote that it was at Mouterhouse that he entered into a serious dialogue with Roman Catholics for the first time. [7] In the preparatory discussions there had been considerable disagreement about whether or not silent meditation should be part of the programme. Finally Fr Hebert was asked to lead a silent retreat with the whole group. Not everyone appreciated this; Visser 't Hooft and Maury "fled" and went for a walk together!

Today we find it hard to imagine how exceptional such an international study retreat was in 1932, bringing together well-known leaders of the major Christian confessions. In the Paris region similar fully ecumenical study-retreats continued to meet, but even within the ecumenically pioneering history of the WSCF five years went by before a second such retreat could be organized in 1937 and then a third in 1939; Jacques Maritain and the Dominican ecumenist Fr Yves Congar participated in both of them.

By then ecumenism was definitely on the agenda of the WSCF and Suzanne's contributions in this field continued throughout the 1930s. At the WSCF general committee meetings at Chamcoria, Bulgaria, in 1935, and at Bièvres in 1937 she presented reports on ecumenism. She was asked to write the WSCF grey book on *The Ecumenical Task of the Student Christian Movement*, which appeared in 1938. It describes the ecumenical pilgrimage of the WSCF, explains the accepted ecumenical policies, and makes suggestions for future work. Immediately after the IMC assembly at Tambaram, India, in 1938 a further ecumenical discussion took place at the WSCF conference in Alwaye, South India. Although Suzanne did not attend that meeting, she was asked to write another WSCF grey book on the basis of the extensive notes taken by the participants. It appeared in 1939 under the title *Students, the Church and the Churches*. Suzanne was also ecumenically active in her position as a member of the executive committee of the World YWCA and as a part-time YWCA staff person. From 1936 she was a member of the group which planned the early joint ventures of all ecumenical youth movements (YMCA, YWCA, WSCF and the youth working group of the future WCC), leading up to the first world conference of Christian youth in Amsterdam just before the outbreak of war in 1939.

Suzanne's own thinking on the work for Christian unity is best expressed in the paper on "The Bible and Ecumenism" which she presented at the second ecumenical retreat in 1937. She began with the warning: "The Bible never offers ready-made answers to any of our questions. Because 'faith' is a dynamic, not a static reality, because we are always faced with the absolute of God's claim and calling on the one hand, and the world-as-it-is on the other, the full answer to any problem will always be paradoxical — thoroughly realistic, and yet charged with expectancy, the expectancy of faith, 'a firm conviction of things not seen', yet already *given*, actual and real."[8]

On the question of unity this basic conviction is then developed in four paradoxical affirmations:

"The Bible knows of a man-made and a God-given unity." Suzanne recalled the parallelism between the stories of the tower of Babel and of Pentecost, and asked whether the ecumenical movement is not tempted hastily to pull together a united front. "The Bible faces us here with its unshakeable realism, and tells us that man-made unity ends in confusion. And once unity is broken, it can be restored only from above."

"The Bible knows of a God-given inclusiveness, and of a God-imposed exclusiveness." This has to do with the inclusiveness of love and the exclusiveness of truth. Thus, although our vocation as revealed in the Bible is one of unity, the process may sometimes be marked by separation, as is evident in the writings of the great prophets of the ninth and eighth centuries before Christ and Paul's struggle against syncretism in the Graeco-Roman world.

"The Bible knows of an exclusiveness which is of God and of an exclusiveness which is of men." It is God's right to separate, not ours. Sectarianism begins when the "faithful" take upon themselves the initiative for separation. Suzanne illustrated this with the way the struggle between exclusive tendencies in the Jerusalem church and Paul is resolved: through an agreement, *not* through mutual concession, but because each of them acknowledges that the other has received his calling from *God*. "Every true ecumenical experience is an opening of our eyes to the reality of our common calling in Christ Jesus."

"The unity of the church of God is both a fact and a promise." We confess in the creed that we believe in the one, catholic church. This is a truth to be accepted in faith but at the same time a goal to pray and suffer for. "At the root of all ecumenical endeavour there must be nothing less than a conversion of heart and mind for all concerned." We should be able to see all things no longer from our own perspective, but from the perspective of God's kingdom.

Suzanne then indicated some practical steps to be taken on this narrow road to unity.

Praying together

"Our Lord left many instructions to his disciples; but on the unity of the church He did not speak; He *prayed*." According to Christ's prayer unity is not a "gentlemen's agreement" among Christians but means entering into the mystery of the triune God: "that they may all be one. As you, Father, are in me and I in you, may they also be in us." At the same time unity implies witness: "so that the world may believe that you have sent me" (John 17:21).

Such unity indeed calls for prayer. The biblical renewal, the search for the message, the rediscovery of the church and the ecumenical quest for unity, all led in the 1930s to a strong liturgical emphasis in the WSCF. One big step had already been taken. In 1924 the first edition of the multilingual and interconfessional WSCF hymnal *Cantate Domino* appeared, prepared by Suzanne Bidgrain. With every new edition it was expanded, and for many student generations singing these hymns became an important part of their ecumenical education. However, worship services at ecumenical gatherings continued to follow an essentially Protestant and revivalist pattern, with free prayers which ignored the rich liturgical heritage of the different confessions.

At the WSCF summer conference in August 1934 an experiment was made which shaped ecumenical worship life for many years to come. The conference took place at La Châtaigneraie, not far from Geneva and near the present Ecumenical Institute at Bossey, and was a highly theological one, where European, North American and Asian participants entered into critical dialogue with Karl Barth. However, the lasting impact of this conference did not come from the theological discussions. Reporting on it, Visser 't Hooft wrote that the notable difference between this and former conferences was "that the day's programme began with a period of Bible study, followed by discussion in groups and that it ended with a liturgical service", something which "had not been tried in a larger international conference". It was a step forward in our common spiritual life "that instead of discussing 'in the air' we discussed the book, the message of which holds us together, and that instead of listening to more 'talk' at the end of the day, we worshipped together through the great classical prayers and hymns of the church".[9] Every evening in a small village church the participants attended a carefully prepared liturgical worship of one confession after another, leading up to a closing worship with a specially prepared ecumenical liturgy. No fully ecumenical prayer and worship books existed at that time, and the organizers were conscious of being "engaged in the exploration of unknown territory". Somebody had to do the preparatory work, and Suzanne was asked to do it.

In 1933 the WSCF executive committee had decided to issue an ecumenical prayerbook to complement *Cantate Domino*. An editorial group was in place, chaired by Suzanne, but little had been done. So in June-July 1934 she went with a pile of liturgical books to Mouterhouse on a working retreat. There she prepared all the liturgies for the Châtaigneraie conference, and these became the basis for the future prayer book *Venite Adoremus*. The ten letters exchanged between Visser 't Hooft and Suzanne during this period give a vivid picture of this creative labour. "I live in the small 'oratoire' [the prayer-room which had been installed in the attic of the house in Mouterhouse for the 1932 retreat], surrounded by papers and liturgies, happy as a mouse in cheese." "I regret that La Châtaigneraie does not last for two weeks. I would have enough material to nourish you each evening and the choice would be less difficult." During these weeks Suzanne laboured, "full of passion for this liturgical work". Every detail — the choice of hymns, scripture readings, the inclusion or exclusion of this or that prayer, the sequence of the different liturgies in relation to the rest of the conference programme, the worship leaders and the typographical presentation of the liturgies — was discussed in the correspondence. Each liturgy was not to last more than thirty minutes. "I am beginning to think that next year we must have a conference centred on the liturgy."

The liturgical material was later checked by members of the various confessions, rewritten and expanded. *Venite Adoremus I* appeared in 1937, the texts printed side by side in English, French and German. It includes the liturgy of the French Reformed Church, the high mass of the Swedish Lutheran Church, the evensong of the Church of England, the Orthodox Easter Vespers and the Complines from the Benedictine Breviary, as well as a collection of early Christian prayers and psalms for different occasions. *Venite Adoremus II* came out in 1938 separately in English, French and German. It contains specially written liturgical material for preparing services at student meetings, camps and conferences, including seven prayers written by Suzanne. Among the "services for different occasions" there are, for instance, those for an act of dedication, for social justice, for times of strife and suffering, and for preparation for holy communion.

It is significant that no eucharistic service is included. "This is deliberate," says the preface to *Venite Adoremus I*. "We recognize that the liturgical services included in this book express only part of the worship of the churches represented and that the crown of such worship is the sacrament of holy communion... The omission does not imply any lack of realization of the crucial importance of this sacrament as the central act of Christian worship, but rather implies the recognition that this very centrality precludes experimentation." [10] Members of different traditions should take the opportunity of attending each other's services of holy communion and seek to enter into the worship of their fellow Christians, without taking communion when doing so is against the discipline of their church.

The pattern of the Châtaigneraie conference with its sequence of Bible study, group meetings, lectures and evening worship shaped the programmes of many future ecumenical gatherings, especially those of the world conferences of Christian youth. Together with *Cantate Domino*, the prayer books *Venite Adoremus* were widely used not only in WSCF meetings but later also in the daily worship life of the Ecumenical Institute at Bossey and meetings of the WCC. What began in the silence of Suzanne's "monastic period" at Mouterhouse has had an impact worldwide.

Witnessing together

With all her enthusiasm for the worship life of the church Suzanne never forgot her evangelistic commitment as a volunteer for Christ. The message commits one to mission. The church is called to witness, and church unity is itself for restoring the wholeness of humanity and all of creation. "Oikoumene" after all does not refer to the whole church but to the whole inhabited earth. The biblical testimony is clear: "In her hope, in her prayers the church shares in the all-inclusive love of God, and ceaselessly waits for the consummation of the ages when God will be 'all in all'." [11]

Suzanne's report on "Evangelization" in 1926 pointed out that students favoured the approach of evangelization through the radiation of the word from the spiritual community. They had little enthusiasm for the earlier method of "evangelization by conquest". After the message study this was not forgotten. Yet there was a new enthusiasm for witnessing by word. What was needed was not a new type of Christian apologetics but obedience to the call "to carry the whole message of the Bible to the whole student". Evangelism in one's own country and foreign mission were seen together within the mission of the church. From 1932 onwards several "missions to the university" took place in Great Britain, the European continent, and Asia and Australasia. Suzanne herself was much involved in preparing the mission to the Latin quarter in January 1933 where Visser 't Hooft, Maury, Berdyaev and André Philip were among the main speakers.

This practice of witnessing led to a new process of reflection. In September 1935 the International Student Conference on Missions was held in Basel, the first large meeting which the WSCF devoted exclusively to the missionary vocation of the church. Its daily programme followed the pattern of La Châtaigneraie, and among the speakers were some of the great leaders of the later world mission conference in Tambaram 1938, for instance the Dutch missionary strategist Hendrik Kraemer and the evangelist D.T. Niles from Ceylon. After attending the conference Suzanne wrote to Visser 't Hooft: "For me Basel has been a strong call to prayer; I was struck by the extent of our responsibilities, by the amazing possibilities which open up before us if we are faithful."

Suzanne summed up what mission meant for her in a meditation at the Fédé congress in 1933. She linked worship and witness closely. The talk was inspired by Pierre de Bérulle, and it would have taken some courage to reaffirm before a mainly Protestant audience the thoughts of this founder of a Roman Catholic order at the time of the counter-Reformation in France. Just before leaving for a mission to England, de Bérulle said to the Oratorian priests: "In all times we have to worship God, for himself and for his works, above all for the greatest of his works which is the incarnation of his Son. But we must do it particularly when He uses us for his service. Therefore we now have to worship God who sent his Son into the world, because this is what consecrates all other missions." [12] Commenting on this Suzanne developed a concept of mission which anticipates much of what in the ecumenical discussions of the 1950s was called the *missio Dei*.

First Suzanne underlined that all participate in God's mission through his Son. All are called to mission. De Bérulle therefore told the Oratorians remaining in France that through their prayers they too would be in England. The true unity of Christian fellowship is based on a common vocation, and such a spiritual community has the power of "'radiation', of 'holy contagion' by a faith and love which by their very nature communicate themselves". The Federation will be dynamic "to the extent it collectively takes cognizance of this mission of witness and intercession". Suzanne recalled her experience of the recent mission to the Latin quarter and added: "It is only our limited faith which limits the possibilities of God."

Second, Suzanne sounded a warning to those involved in such missions: they may only seek themselves through their evangelistic activities. What they do must become a reflection of the great mission of God through the mystery of the incarnation. This means not only "daring to believe, daring to say that God's descent into history is the unique event which gives meaning to the whole of this history"; the incarnation also shows us the mode of God's action: the word is made flesh. To participate in this mission means "to leave one's self for becoming others through the all-powerful miracle of love". "Thus each mission is a continuing incarnation of the supernatural obedience of the Son from one stage to the other, from the desert to calvary." It is then no longer a matter "of proclaiming the truth, but of living the truth".

NOTES

[1] N.P. Grubb, quoted in P. Gruner, *Gotteswege und Menschenwege im Studentenleben*, Bern, 1942, p.383.

[2] M. Boegner, *L'exigence œcuménique*, Paris, 1968, p.39.

[3] Mayr, *Einheit und Botschaft*, I, pp.227-63, with full bibliography on the message study in II A, pp.77-91.

[4] SdD, "A Tentative History of the Federation Message", *The Student World*, 1931, pp.116f.

[5] SdD, "Le siècle de l'Eglise"; "Réflexions sur un thème: Qu'est-ce que l'Eglise?"; "L'Eglise 'corps du Christ' dans la piété paulinienne", all in *Le semeur*, November 1930, pp.41-47; July 1931, pp.405-26; and February 1933, pp.195-205.

[6] SdD and Henry-Louis Henriod, "The Ecumenical Task of the Federation", *The Student World*, 1933, pp.23f.

[7] W.A. Visser 't Hooft, *Memoirs*, Geneva, WCC, 1973, pp.66f.

[8] SdD, "The Bible and Ecumenism", *The Student World*, 1937, pp.114ff.

[9] W.A. Visser 't Hooft, "Editor's Travel Diary", *The Student World*, 1934, pp.349f.

[10] "Preface", *Venite Adoremus I*, pp.7f. This preface was already adopted by the WSCF general committee in Chamcoria, 1935.

[11] SdD, "The Bible and Ecumenism", p.119.

[12] SdD, "Mission", *Le semeur*, April/May 1933, pp.51,53,54,56ff.

8
Prophetic Service

September 1921: Suzanne was back in Reichshoffen, physically and mentally exhausted. She worried over the war, and then about the peace. She suffered from rheumatism and had to submit to another session of hydrotherapy. A new development in the de Dietrich factories affected her deeply: the workers had gone on strike. She wrote to Jean B. Couve who served as a volunteer for Christ among mine-workers in the north of France: "When will the gospel be the leaven in the lump? It always seems that the leaven is on one side and the lump on the other."

The complexity of the socio-economic situation baffled Suzanne. She realized that both owners and workers were caught in the power play of their associations and unions. The discussions on social justice in student circles now looked so naive. She would have liked to see the members of the Fédé in the position of an industrial boss struggling to keep his business alive when faced with increasing demands from workers. She could not help thinking that this would have been her lot, had she chosen the way of Christoph Dieterlen and not that of Tommy Fallot. Having spoken and written much about the Christian faith, she now decided she had enough of "'spoken' Christianity"!

Words and acts

With her complete honesty and abhorrence of hypocrisy, Suzanne was acutely aware of this ever-present gap between faith and life. In her journals she sometimes comes across as very insecure, constantly accusing herself of shortcomings and weaknesses. In 1921 she had just published her first article on the prophets, and she was preparing a series of studies on the prophetic message. She was struck by the fact that the prophets not only speak, they act. In their lives God's word manifests itself with the same word-event unity which marks the creation story: "And God said..., and it was so."

She had learned from her spiritual ancestors of Ban de la Roche, and she had read the Christian socialists Hermann Kutter and Leonhard

Ragaz. It was not surprising, then, that she was now ready to hear the prophetic voice of Walter Rauschenbusch, the leader of the social gospel movement in America. His book on *The Social Principles of Jesus* appeared in 1918 and she freely adapted Rauschenbusch's view of the prophetic Jesus for high-school students. All this, however, was simply writing, speaking, teaching. What about prophetic *acts*?

Suzanne did a great deal behind the scenes. A large part of her time and energy was spent on the work and financing for the international student foyer in Paris. She helped the Fédé to survive financially through gifts and loans and by organizing fund-raising campaigns. The house in Mouterhouse was made available not only for the Fédé but also as a vacation centre for foreign students. She regularly visited students suffering from tuberculosis who were treated in Leysin, Switzerland. When in 1925 Suzanne moved into her own apartment in Paris, it became a home not only for the children of her sister Amélie, but also for women students who needed the reassuring presence of someone who understood them. From the letters she received we can see how much she helped friends in need, foreigners whom she hardly knew and the families of her sisters. Despite all this, Suzanne remained only too well aware of the disparity between her strong social consciousness and her relatively affluent situation. She never renounced material possessions, but she once confided: "There is a problem with being well off, and all my life it has remained insoluble. What does it mean to be poor? I can never be quite at ease when I read certain passages of the gospel. I always ask myself what it means to go to the limits set by the gospel. I do not know..." [1]

"The truth to serve"

Once again we need to go back to the WSCF meeting at Beatenberg in 1920, for Suzanne's developing socio-political thought and attitude to service were marked by what she experienced in the Federation. Besides preserving its unity in faith, this worldwide fellowship of students had to decide how it could respond to the political tensions and human needs of the post-war period. The three basic objectives stated in the WSCF constitution — Christian faith and life, Bible study and evangelization — were not in question. At Beatenberg two further objectives were added: the WSCF was "to bring students of all countries into mutual understanding and sympathy, to lead them to realize that the principles of Jesus Christ should rule in international relationships, and to endeavour by so doing to draw the nations together"; and it was "to further, either directly or indirectly, the efforts on behalf of the welfare of students in body, mind and spirit which are in harmony with the Christian purpose". [2]

Suzanne voted in favour. She fully supported the intention of the two additions; they corresponded to the war experience of the French volunteers for Christ and to her own passionate belief in political and social involvement. In accordance with the last objective, the Beatenberg committee decided that the WSCF should take full responsibility for European student relief, and Suzanne immediately became active in this area of WSCF work.

The international aim of the Federation reflected the ideals of US President Woodrow Wilson and the North American enthusiasm for building a new world order, which some people almost identified with God's kingdom. The recently founded League of Nations, it was hoped, would be undergirded by Christian social ethics. Behind this sociopolitical commitment was also the belief that "doctrine divides while service unites", which was one of the assumptions of the world conference of the Life and Work movement at Stockholm in 1925. That service does not always unite was experienced painfully by the WSCF two years after Beatenberg at its general committee meeting in Peking. Discussion on international aims soon gave rise to passionate debate and disagreement. The fellowship could be maintained only by agreeing to disagree on questions of pacifism, actions with regard to race relations and concrete political involvement. In fact, only after the "message study" of 1929-32 developed a new, biblically-based thinking on social ethics could the WSCF have a basis for common social action and students find the "the truth to serve", as W.A. Visser 't Hooft entitled his first five years' report as WSCF general secretary.

Recalling that time, Suzanne later wrote: "The proclamation of the lordship of Christ over all realms of life meant that no aspect of daily life, in home and factory, economics and politics, art and science could be ignored. All things took their ultimate significance in God's creative and redeeming action as revealed in Christ. This message came as a gift of God, at the very moment when totalitarian systems tried to circumscribe the Christian message to the sphere of 'private life' or tried to make use of the church for their own purposes; at a time when the Marxist interpretation of history attracted thousands of young people, in East and West. This all-embracing vision of God's purpose for his world necessarily implied a new vision of the mission of the church. The church had stood all too long on the defensive, abandoning sphere after sphere of life to the secular world. She had now to stand up and claim the whole of life for

Christ with joyful boldness."[3] The WSCF further defined its thought on "the nature of Christian social action" at a conference at Swanwick, Great Britain, in 1935. In many respects it anticipated the findings of the much larger, more official Life and Work conference at Oxford in 1937 with its watchword: "Let the church be the church".

Suzanne was present neither in Peking nor at Swanwick, but she followed this development of socio-political thought and action with great interest. She assiduously read and contributed to the WSCF journal *The Student World* which in the 1932-35 period published theme numbers on "Disarmament", "The End of the Bourgeois", "The Christian and the Nation", "The Call to Revolution" and "Our Attitude to the 'Next War'". At the 1935 WSCF general committee in Chamcoria, Bulgaria, she voted for the statement "that the most vital contribution the Federation can make in the present atmosphere of international tension is to hold together in one Christian community those who are divided politically and nationally, and to deepen understanding between nations. This task is to be fulfilled without ignoring or condemning national and political loyalties." Suzanne was a WSCF representative at the Oxford world conference in 1937 which confirmed her conviction that the church can fulfill its task only if laymen and laywomen become mature Christians and are the church in their daily life and professions.

War was raging in China and in Spain. What was happening in the Baltic and the Balkan states as well as the threats to Czechoslovakia filled Suzanne with much concern. In June 1938 she was an eye-witness of something which influenced much of what she later wrote and did: on the very day she was a guest in the home of Jewish friends in Berlin, the two daughters of the family had to flee to England to escape being caught in Nazi raids. The theme "the righteousness of men and the righteousness of God" was now ever-present in Suzanne's mind. She had conducted a study on this subject at the WSCF Bible conference in 1937 at Bièvres, basing it on the sermon on the mount. She also agreed to write on the delicate question: "War rather than Injustice?" for a *Student World* issue on international order in 1939. But before that article was written, political events forced her to leave the realm of academic discussion and to enter the public arena of controversial debate.

Munich 1938: a prophetic protest

"Are there decisive times when, like an individual, a whole people will sell its soul to save its life? I believe there are."[4] With these words Suzanne started her controversial prophetic protest against what had happened in Munich during the night of 29-30 September 1938. France and Britain had guaranteed the frontiers of Czechoslovakia, but that night both the French and the British prime ministers ceded yet again to Hitler's territorial claims. They allowed the German Reich to incorporate the Sudetenland in northern Bohemia, hoping thereby to secure peace.

On that fateful night Suzanne was still working for the World YWCA, on her fifth visit to North America. In mid-September she wrote to Visser 't Hooft from New York about her fear that Czechoslovakia might soon become another Spain and about the German canons directed against her beloved Alsace. A few days later she saw the newspaper headline: "French Betrayal". Then came the news about Munich.

Suzanne immediately decided to return to France. What she saw when she got back early in October disgusted her. Instead of mourning over the betrayal of Czechoslovakia, most people seemed relieved, and thankful for the "peace". Both the French nationalist and the prophetic Christian in Suzanne exploded. What came from her pen spared neither her country nor her Christians compatriots, neither the political left nor the bourgeoisie "who today lick the boots of Hitler". "Politically, the bottom line is clear this September: with the consent of France and Great Britain a policy of gangsterism has been established in Europe. True, this policy was not born yesterday. We have seen it operate elsewhere; but it is the first time it does so with our consent. Humanly speaking the Munich agreements are probably better than war. Morally this is not so certain; no peace can be built on betrayal. If our air defence had allowed us to speak to Hitler on a level of equality we might not have had a Munich.... [France] is the country that has been defeated with the Munich agreement. The whole world sees and knows it. I am not concerned about our 'prestige', which has to do only with human grandeur. But for all small nations of the earth the word of France no longer counts." Then follows the prediction that all small nations east of the Berlin-Rome axis will be annexed to the German Reich and that this will most probably not be the end of it.

Having drawn up this political "balance sheet", Suzanne commented on the inadequacies of Christians. What troubled her most was the ease with which they shouted "peace, peace" while there was no peace (Ezek. 13:10 and Mark 8:35 formed the basic text of her protest). "We had neither the courage for peace (1920-33) nor the courage for war (1933-38). We failed to recognize the fundamental Christian position which affirms that there is no peace without justice." Conceding that the 1938 situation was partly caused by the injustices of the Treaty of Versailles,

Suzanne refused to accept this as a justification for new unjust treaties. She recalled what the Israelite prophets had said about corrupt political alliances. The French-British abandonment of Czechoslovakia at Munich reminded her of the verse: "That same day [namely, the day they sentenced the innocent Jesus to death] Herod and Pilate became friends" (Luke 23:12). The prophetic protest ends with an appeal to Christians in France: "We must free ourselves from fear. A Christian knows that empires collapse but God remains... For Christians in Europe a time of testing will begin and no one yet knows how serious it will be and how long it will last. The irreducible antagonism between totalitarian regimes and Christian faith has been amply demonstrated... As the rule of Hitler is gradually established in Europe, Christians will be called to abdicate or to suffer. We must prepare ourselves and gather our forces for the struggle, for we do not know when our turn will come... But we, Christians and French, must also remember that *before God* we are responsible for the destiny of our country and we must not let it go downhill without resisting. Too often we have taken refuge in pious absenteeism. Let us enter the civic strife, but enter it as persons for whom God's kingdom and its justice are primary; as persons who judge the affairs of the time with common sense because they view them in the perspective of eternity."

In Protestant France this was the first clear public condemnation of the Munich agreements. Soon others joined the debate and Suzanne received many responses. "Finally, what needed to be said has been said." A conscientious objector wrote to her commending what she had written: "When faced with evil I have never identified non-violence with passivity."

However, there were other highly critical responses, some of which must have brought Suzanne much sorrow and soul-searching. Paul Evdokimov was deeply shocked: "I must say with the whole strength of my conviction that for me the tone of your entire article is not at all Christian." The professor of law and theological thinker Jacques Ellul wrote a letter to the editor of *Le semeur*. He accused Suzanne of confusing God's peace and justice with the human understanding of peace and justice; he pointed to the complexity and the ambiguities of all human struggles; he alleged that she had used scripture wrongly. This last point provoked Suzanne to publish a rejoinder. Ezekiel 13:10 spoke not only about peace with God, as Ellul affirmed, but also about the false temporal security of the Israelites who had stayed on in Jerusalem. Such prophetic warnings of the Old Testament also had implications for present-day politics. For reasons of state Herod and Pilate condemned an innocent man to death, and their friendship was based on that complicity. This was her point, and not an identification of Czechoslovakia with Christ, as Ellul made out. Suzanne saw the same kind of complicity in the French-German pact signed in December 1938, "the day after most appalling anti-semitic persecutions". Suzanne admitted that divine and human justice must not be confused, but "the vocation of the state, as described in Romans 13, is to maintain order and justice. However relative such human justice may be, it is nevertheless a clear mandate from God. I believe it is this mandate which our governments have betrayed, and the duty of Christians is to say so." Suzanne totally rejected Ellul's affirmation that in our sinful world the difference between the regimes in Germany and France was only relative. [5]

The paper on "War rather than Injustice?" which Suzanne wrote soon after for *The Student World* presented her position in a more balanced way. In her first article on the prophets Suzanne had placed side by side three formidable dispensers of justice and judgment: Amos, John the Baptist and the prophetic figure of Brand, taken from one of Henrik Ibsen's plays. Brand took as the voice of God what was only the voice of pride, and Suzanne commented: "The characteristic of the prophet is to be humble; the characteristic of a false prophet is that he always ends up by deifying himself; in his final hours of hallucination Brand believed he was the Messiah. The prophet accepts the possibility of failure, for he is the objective witness of somebody else and his role is only to testify; success and failure are the concerns of God. The false prophet wants to succeed. He is haunted by any compromise. Defeated, he descends into madness." [6] Such distinctions can easily be made on paper and with the example of a false prophet from fiction, but now Suzanne is accused as one herself. The Bible gives no clear criteria to distinguish true prophecy from false in a particular historical context. Subsequent events proved that Suzanne was right in much of her protest, but in 1938 the situation was by no means clear. Once again she had to rely totally on God's grace and divine forgiveness.

Amsterdam 1939: a prophetic sign

"If *this* is possible, I can't continue to think that the world is lost." An Amsterdam town counsellor expressed his amazement at what happened in his city from 24 July to 2 August 1939, four weeks before the outbreak of the second world war. In fact, what happened was simply another world conference, which by now was not an extraordinary event any more. This time it was the first Christian world youth conference. Perhaps the counsellor was right. This particular gathering of almost 1600 delegates and official visitors from some seventy countries and all continents became a prophetic sign. The conference also summed up much of Suzanne's work in the 1920s and 1930s, although her name does not appear on the programme. She had been an active member of the preparatory committee and she helped to shape the theme, the daily schedule, the worship and especially the Bible studies. But she never appeared on the platform.

The official announcement of the event was made in 1937: "The conference will gather representative young members and leaders of the youth work of the churches and of all national and international Christian youth movements. It aims at confronting youth with the results of the world gatherings of the Christian churches and the Christian youth movements in the years 1937 and 1938. Its purpose is to mobilize youth to witness to the reality of the Christian community as the God-given supra-national body to which has been entrusted the message of the victory of Jesus Christ over the world's spiritual, political and social confusion."[7] A more official church ecumenism was gaining momentum and the decision to create a World Council of Churches had already been taken, but only relatively few, and mainly male, leaders in church, mission and theology were involved. Younger men and women, more lay people and more people from outside Europe and North America were needed. Since 1936 the YMCA, YWCA and WSCF had worked together for conferences of Christian workers among boys and girls, held at Dassel, Germany. These movements were asked to send half the total number of participants to Amsterdam; the other half was to consist of representatives of church youth groups in Protestant and Orthodox churches. Roman Catholics still did not have permission from the church hierarchy to attend. From Germany only a few participants were able to come, and secretly. For the first time all the agencies of the ecumenical movement collaborated: the YMCA, the YWCA and the WSCF, the International Missionary Council, the movements of Life and Work and Faith and Order, the World Alliance for International Friendship through the Churches, and the World Sunday School Association.

Suzanne was asked to propose texts and suggest methods for the Bible study at the conference. In 1938 she presented the outlines, which were accepted with minor changes. The daily Bible study period was put in between a major lecture and the afternoon special interest groups, and the texts were chosen in relation to the themes of the discussion groups. This was to become a feature of many future ecumenical Bible studies: they were not an isolated exercise of biblical piety before the burning questions of the church's task in the world were faced; they were at the centre of the programme, questioning and informing the work of the meeting. At a two-day preparatory meeting for speakers, moderators and group leaders immediately before the conference, Suzanne introduced the Bible studies and conducted a training session with the leaders.

The daily schedule of the meeting was similar to the pattern developed for the La Châtaigneraie student conference. In many of the evaluations received from participants two programme items emerged as especially significant: the worship services and the Bible study periods. What Suzanne had done single-handedly for the worship at La Châtaigneraie was now done much more systematically by groups representing various liturgical traditions. Both through distributed printed liturgies with explanatory introductions and through their actual participation in the services, people received a thorough liturgical and ecumenical education. Besides the opening and closing worships they took part in an Irish free church service, a French Reformed and a Hungarian Lutheran morning service, and less confessional worship forms developed in different cultural milieus and led by a South African Bantu woman, an Indian Christian and a group of North Americans. There was also a special service of preparation for the holy communion, after which participants attended a Dutch Reformed, a Lutheran and an Anglican holy communion service as well as an Orthodox liturgy. No one could fully partake in all these eucharistic celebrations, and the scandalously visible disunity of Christians at the Lord's table led many participants to a renewed commitment to work for unity. The one uniting link in these various worship services was the hymn book *Cantate Domino*.

A major criticism was that the Amsterdam conference had been prepared and directed by old, mostly male, leaders and that the youth participants had little opportunity to speak for themselves. Even in the afternoon special interest sessions the presence of invited "experts" in each group might have stifled free discussion by ordinary youth participants. This, however, was not true of the Bible study groups where all the members discussed the biblical text and challenged one another's dogmatic presuppositions. Not all of the 42 groups went well. There were occasions when the theological students seemed to claim the "expert" role. The final conference statement said: "We believe that those who planned this conference were guided by God when they placed Bible study in such a central place. Many of us have discovered the Bible afresh, and in so far as we have allowed God to speak to us, He has become a living God, declaring a living message for our lives and our generation. We confess, however, to our humiliation, that our study has revealed considerable unfamiliarity with the Bible... Real Bible study must lead to definite choices and decisions in all areas of life. To listen to God means to obey him."[8]

It is significant that the first post-Amsterdam publication sent to the participants, in response to their special request, was a Bible study booklet entitled *The Faith which Overcomes the World*, written after the conference by Visser 't Hooft and Suzanne. Some 180 delegates from SCMs in all parts of the world met after Amsterdam at a WSCF conference in Nunspeet, Holland, where Suzanne led a series of studies on the book of the prophet Jeremiah.

The theme of the Amsterdam youth assembly, "Christus Victor", may sound triumphalistic, but one must remember the desperate world situation at the time. In June-July 1939 the organizers were on the verge of calling off the whole enterprise. But to meet around such a theme at such a time was like the prophetic sign of Jeremiah who bought a piece of land during the siege of Jerusalem when the nation had already lost their land (Jer. 32). To acclaim Christ as the Victor when Hitler dictated the course of world history meant really to "let the church be the church". At that critical hour the fundamental political Christian testimony was to gather, in the face of demonic powers, a universal Christian community, to empower it, and to confess: Christ is the ultimately victorious Lord. Years later, many participants testified that Amsterdam had shaped their view of the world and marked their life subsequently. Even Visser 't Hooft, who was probably involved in more ecumenical gatherings than anyone else, wrote: "I do not believe that any large ecumenical conference has been so completely timely and relevant or has had such direct influence on the life of the delegates."[9]

CIMADE: a prophetic service

"Where all feel safe, the prophet forecasts doom; where all despair the prophet hopes and speaks a word of consolation." In early August 1939 Suzanne said that about Jeremiah's prophetic purchase of land, concluding: "The message of the prophets is summarized in one word: repentance. Repentance means changing our ways... I am no prophet. I do not know if God's way will be peace or war for the Europe of tomorrow. What I know is that we should pray for true repentance and for postponement of judgment. But at the same time we must be ready to stand under God's judgment when it comes and under whatever form it comes." There is a final essential lesson to be learned from the prophetic teaching:

"When all human doors of escape close on us, God opens 'a door of hope'. Over the chaos of our world his tremendous reality stands, ever righteous and merciful; all the greater for our littleness; the one reality on which we can stake our all. And what the prophets dimly saw, we know: over the raging battlefields his cross stands, with ever outstretched arms." [10] On 1 September the German armies invaded Poland. France and Great Britain began to mobilize, determined this time to keep their promises. When Hitler did not respond to their ultimatum, on 3 September Britain and France declared war on the German Reich.

Meanwhile Suzanne had returned to Geneva after a six-month period of travel and conferences. Tired and ill, she was very depressed. She had looked forward to working with the Alsatian biblical theologian Théo Preiss who had been welcomed as a new WSCF secretary at the Nunspeet meeting, but before he could begin his assignment he had to go and serve at the front. In the last extant letter from Suzanne to Marguerite Ecoffey, she wrote from Geneva in September 1939: "Ever since I came back here my thoughts have remained on the other side of the frontier except during the hours I concentrate on my work." Soon she left again for France to consult in Paris and Bièvres with the remaining leaders of French Protestant youth movements, knowing full well that all able-bodied men between 20 and 49 would have joined the forces and that the movements would face acute financial problems. She was also concerned over the fate of the evacuated Alsatians. The military authorities had prepared a plan to transfer a considerable number of French citizens living near the strategic Maginot line in Alsace-Lorraine to central and south-western France. This plan was never fully carried out, but during the chaotic days of the mobilization in early September the whole population of Strasbourg and of many villages in northern Alsace had been evacuated, among them a large number of Protestants.

Suzanne had already written to Mrs Jacques Pannier who presided over both the French YWCA and a coordinating body of French Protestant youth movements, about the need to organize coordinated action for those evacuated. From Bièvres she wrote to Preiss: "I think our youth movements should get together to help the Alsatian refugees in the four or five regions where they have been sent. I feel really worried about it... Marc Boegner is most concerned about this question and he has suggested I go to the Dordogne where the situation is most difficult and where the people from Strasbourg are." Others were equally concerned. Charles Gouillon, a French pastor who worked at the headquarters of the World YMCA in Geneva, visited south-west France to find out how the YMCAs could help. The French scouts had been involved in receiving the refugees. Suzanne was impressed by people's readiness to work together. More than fifty youth representatives from the French churches and movements had been at the Amsterdam conference, and the common vision was beginning to bear fruit.

On 18 October at a meeting of the various French Protestant youth movements in Bièvres it was decided to launch joint action. Together with Georgette Siegrist, an experienced leader of the French Federation of girl scouts, Suzanne was asked to make a survey of the needs. They travelled to the Dordogne and on to the Pyrenees. In the south-west they joined forces with a YMCA secretary. On the basis of this exploratory journey Suzanne wrote a travel report and a memorandum [11] which became the basic documents for the creation of CIMADE, the Comité inter-mouvements auprès des évacués (Inter-movement Committee for Evacuees).

The situations in which the refugees from Alsace found themselves varied greatly. Some had already been relatively well settled, especially where a whole village community could stay together. There were examples of growing solidarity between the Lutherans and the Reformed among the refugees and between the displaced Protestants and some resident Catholics. Nevertheless, the majority of refugees still lived in primitive conditions, and often felt totally lost. These were mostly Protestant factory workers and city-dwellers, now forced to live in one of the poorest rural areas and among very conservative Catholics. No real contact was possible because the Alsatians spoke their Germanic dialect, and even those who understood French could not follow the French dialect of the rural population. Other Alsatians had been assigned to villages which had already given refuge to fugitives from the Spanish civil war. There was a real danger that many refugees, including the young ones, would become apathetic. The survey team made proposals for action: mobile teams of Christian youth leaders and social workers, each including a member who spoke Alsatian, should be sent to the regions where there were refugees. The young people should be brought together and organized to do social and religious work; this would give them a sense of purpose.

These proposals were accepted. In November 1939 a team started working in the Dordogne, among them Siegrist, some YWCA workers and two Alsatian-speaking deaconesses from Strasbourg who had also been evacuated. Suzanne saw to it that the necessary funds were obtained. The Fédé, the scouts and the YWCA organized camps for Alsatian youth in the central region at Christmas time and it was then that CIMADE took shape with Pannier as president and Siegrist as secretary.

All this was certainly a vital service at that hour, but Suzanne saw more lasting gains beyond the immediate need. "It is strange to hear Alsatian spoken on the roads of Périgord" (an area of the Dordogne), she wrote. "This Alsatian population has something to contribute to the other areas of France as well as something to receive." CIMADE teams helped to create a greater understanding between the cultures and ways of life of Alsace and the interior of France. As a volunteer for Christ, Suzanne also hoped that through collaborative social and evangelistic work the gospel would reach milieus with which Protestant youth movements had so far had no contact whatsoever. Such team work would also be the best training for the youth leaders themselves. Day-to-day collaboration among members of the different youth movements was not easy. Already in December 1939 Suzanne had received a letter from the travelling secretary of the Fédé, complaining about difficulties with differing styles of leadership. A few months later the right leader was found in the person of Madeleine Barot, who became the great leader of CIMADE. [12]

As early as October 1939 Suzanne had perceived a much more difficult and costly task ahead. She ended her report by pointing to the large number of civil internees and foreigners living in France for whom help might have to be organized. She did not know then that in less than a year CIMADE would be called on to go into the ill-famed internment camps of Gurs and Rivesaltes near the Pyrenees and to work illegally to save the lives of many Jews.

NOTES

[1] Chambron, interview with SdD, transcript p.23; cc. also pp.11 and 21ff.

[2] Appendix on the constitution of the WSCF in Ruth Rouse, *The World's Student Christian Federation*, London, 1948, pp.314-20.

[3] SdD, "Crisis and Renewal in the Student World", in R.C. Mackie & Charles West, eds, *The Sufficiency of God*, London, 1963, pp.33f.

[4] SdD, "A propos du mois de septembre", *Le semeur*, November 1938, pp.1-7.

[5] SdD, "Réponse à Jacques Ellul", *Le semeur*, February 1939, pp.230-33.

[6] SdD, "Prophètes et faux prophètes", *Le semeur*, November-December 1920, p.109.

[7] *A World Conference of Christian Youth*, first announcement, Geneva, 1937, p.4.

[8] *Christus Victor: The Report of the World Conference of Christian Youth*, Geneva, 1939, pp.238f.

[9] Visser 't Hooft, *Memoirs*, p.103.

[10] SdD, "Three Studies in the Book of Jeremiah", *The Student World*, 1939, pp.322,338f.

[11] SdD, report on a visit in France, 9-31 October 1939, and notes on a journey through the areas of withdrawal for people evacuated from Alsace, October 1939.

[12] André Jacques, *Madeleine Barot: Une indomptable énergie*, Paris, Editions du Cerf, (abridged English ed.: *Madeline Barot*, Geneva, WCC, 1991).

9
A Network of Friendships

That might hardly seem the most appropriate title for a chapter on the second world war. But in the extensive wartime correspondence of Suzanne no word is used more centrally than "friendship". Through the work of movements such as the WSCF, a worldwide network of friendships had grown, and it was now being tested by closed frontiers and actual fighting on opposing fronts. The world conference of youth in Amsterdam had indeed been timely. Even this event could not have maintained the network intact through the following six years had not Suzanne and her colleagues used all their energy in exchanging information and providing material and spiritual support.

This time the war was on a world scale with battlefields in Asia, the Pacific islands, the Middle East and North Africa as well as in Europe. Combatants came from almost all continents and the population of the whole world was affected, even villagers in the mountains of New Guinea who had had no contact with the outside world. In Europe some 26 million people died; 19 percent of the total population of Poland, 10 percent of Yugoslavia, and in actual numbers many more in Russia, Germany and elsewhere. The majority of these were not soldiers but from among the civilian population. There was less hand-to-hand fighting than there had been in the bloody battles of the 1914-18 war: the killing was on a more massive and impersonal scale. It was a "mechanized and scientific war where you kill without even seeing what you are doing", as Théo Preiss wrote to Suzanne; "it is killing by the simple precision of observations, measurements and calculations, where you become out of touch with the 'result' of your 'work'. It is then physically almost impossible to feel concrete personal responsibility. Responsibility is as it were diluted, endlessly divided. There are only 'servants', 'objects' in front, no more human beings on this side or the other. Nevertheless, we are still completely responsible for it." Like others of Suzanne's friends Preiss spent the first month of the war at a look-out post on the Rhine, waiting for the attack. For more than eight months it did not come, and then it was not the canons of the Siegfried line which shattered the Maginot line in Alsace-Lorraine, but German tanks which swept through the Netherlands, Belgium and the Ardennes, crushing the French army in June 1940.

Agents of communication

Little happened at first on the western front and the French spoke of "la drôle de guerre", the "phoney war". In China, Poland, Finland and the Baltic states war was only too real with thousands slaughtered and floods of refugees, but in the West it was a time of waiting. The respite was well used by the WSCF for setting up channels of communication within its network.

Who were the main agents? In France it was still Suzanne Bidgrain. Forced by illness to give up her work as WSCF travelling secretary in 1927, she nevertheless continued to be active, maintaining contact with the SCMs in the Nordic and Baltic countries. She also did much translation work and thus facilitated the flow of information and ideas across language barriers and closed frontiers. Marc Boegner had become a public figure and the relationship between him and Suzanne was now more formal. As the president of the French Protestant Federation he represented the rights, opinions and demands of Protestants vis-a-vis the state, a delicate task when he had to deal with the government of Marshal Pétain in Vichy. Boegner convinced Suzanne in June 1940 that she should go back to her international task in Geneva although she wanted to stay in France and serve her country. Pierre Maury, who had become Boegner's colleague in the parish of Passy in Paris, remained a great support for Suzanne, and so did Charles Westphal, the general secretary of the Fédé now serving in the army.

From September 1939 onwards a team of women carried the main burden of the French SCM: Jeanne Lebrun and Denise Duflo, helped by Claire Jullien who from 1940 worked at the conference centre in Bièvres. From Geneva Suzanne supported this team as much as she could. When at times she felt that the Fédé was not doing justice to its prophetic ministry in the war situation or to its work of serious Bible study, she did not hesitate to admonish her French colleagues.

After the French defeat in 1940 three-fifths of France became the "occupied zone" where regular youth work was no longer possible though Jean Bosc, who stayed in the north, conducted many Bible studies among Protestant youth. In the "free zone" of southern France youth movements could continue to function. In the matter of cooperating with CIMADE and the French Protestant youth council Madeleine Barot was now the main correspondent. Suzanne also worked with the new general secretary of the Fédé, Georges Casalis, and after 1943 with his successor, André Dumas. She remained in contact with the Russian SCM in exile through its secretary, Leon Zander, and she made sure that throughout the war his salary was paid by the WSCF. The disagreement about Munich had in no way lessened her friendship with Paul and Natacha Evdokimov.

Her closest friend in France at this time was Preiss. When in 1940 he was taken prisoner, people from many parts of the world wrote asking for news of him. As an Alsatian he had been freed by the Germans to work as a pastor in occupied Alsace. From there he sent a letter written in German to Geneva. For the censors it contained nothing but harmless family gossip. But it was in actual fact in coded language, giving details of what he did and thought, even announcing his planned escape. After a first abortive attempt Preiss finally managed to reach Switzerland in July 1942; he proceeded to Montpellier where he taught New Testament. From there he helped Suzanne with her biblical training work.

The art of composing and deciphering coded letters now became important. How else could Suzanne keep in contact with Reinhold von Thadden, Hanns Lilje and other members of the disbanded German SCM? All letters to the Allied countries were censored. When postal connections from Switzerland to Britain and North America were cut Birgit Rodhe of the Swedish SCM became the agent of communication between the WSCF office in Geneva and the rest of the world. Francis House, an Anglican priest and Suzanne's colleague on the WSCF staff, could in 1939-40 still visit the student movements in south-eastern Europe. During the German attack on the western front he was in England and could not return to WSCF work until 1944 when he again visited south-eastern Europe. In the interim he was Suzanne's main British correspondent.

Two other WSCF staff colleagues were forced to discontinue their work. Luther Tucker, the secretary for the Far East, was arrested in Japan and for a time imprisoned in Kyoto. T.C. Koo made a long visit to the Indian sub-continent, China, North America and Australia before he was interned by the Japanese in Hong Kong in 1941. He escaped but, caught in the turmoils of the war in China, little was known about him until he returned to WSCF work in 1945. From North America the WSCF treasurer, Ronald Elliott, and the vice-moderator, Helen Morton, maintained contact with Geneva throughout the war. In 1940 Morton was sent on a WSCF visitation to Japan, the Indian sub-continent, China and the Philippines. Just before her departure Suzanne wrote to her: "I was so glad to hear about your going to the Far East. It is a great comfort to think that that part of the world will not be neglected... I find it pretty hard not to be in Paris. I was there all through the last war and not to be there now seems a kind of desertion."

With the same letter Suzanne sent translated excerpts from letters of Preiss so that his friends in the Far East might know his thinking. When in 1942 the Japanese armies advanced in Asia, Suzanne wrote to her colleague Robert C. Mackie: "My thoughts are constantly in the Far East, visiting friend after friend as they too enter the war zone one by one... I got a good letter from Kiang Wen Han (the Asian WSCF vice-moderator) some time ago but there too I suppose the old route is closed." In Latin America the Gallands in Buenos Aires remained the chief contact persons. The wartime travel reports of all these WSCF staff members and officers read rather like a detective novel. [1]

In Geneva Suzanne had the continuing support of Willem Visser 't Hooft. In 1938 he accepted the invitation to become the secretary of the World Council of Churches (WCC) in process of formation. Suzanne was deeply disappointed: "Wim, do you realize what these three years of working together with you have meant for me? I do not know whether I will ever find to such a degree that joy of communion in the work of serving the same truth... It is terrible for me to see you becoming an ecclesiastical 'big shot', for this is a bunch I do not like; but perhaps it will be your humble brothers of the Federation who will save you from becoming the big boss who loves to hear himself talk?" [2] Wim continued as WSCF moderator, and in the increasingly isolated Geneva of 1941 he wrote: "During my regular visits to Suzanne de Diétrich at 13 rue Calvin [the WSCF headquarters], where we study letters and documents from many countries, we feel often surrounded by a cloud of witnesses, but somehow you cannot chair a cloud." In fact, Visser 't Hooft was by then deeply involved in another crucial network, that of church leaders and ecclesiastical resistance movements. [3] Different priorities at times led to disagreements between him and Suzanne. This happened, for instance, during the depressing weeks of September 1942 when the Jews in the detention camps of southern France were being taken to death camps in Poland. At a meeting on student relief Visser 't Hooft wanted a statement to be issued about recent events. Suzanne objected; she was afraid it would jeopardize the work of CIMADE and those in the detention camps. "Wim was a bit angry with me", she wrote, "and told me I had broken 'the Christian front'! I did not take it too seriously. We are so close that it is always painful to disagree but sometimes I have to. Wim has a passion for documents and written statements; of course he needs them in his job."

That letter was addressed to Mackie, since 1938 the general secretary of the WSCF. In the beginning Suzanne wondered whether she would have with him an equally rewarding collaboration as with Visser 't Hooft, but soon Mackie gained her full confidence and friendship. He was a Scot who had fought as a soldier in the 1914-18 war, then served as British SCM secretary and WSCF treasurer. In the first two years of his new assignment he travelled widely in Europe, throughout Asia and North America, visiting SCMs. He thus brought to the Federation a truly worldwide perspective and also special gifts of grace which complemented those of Visser 't Hooft and Suzanne: gifts of discernment, administration and pastoral concern, patience, wisdom and wit. [4]

After her visit to France in October 1939 Suzanne spent a winter of hectic work in Geneva. In March 1940 she again went to France to meet with SCM groups and members of the CIMADE teams. While in the home of her friends the Evdokimovs in Menton she heard the news of the German attack in the north. Reluctantly she returned to Geneva at the end of May.

The Robert-Suzanne team

"No news from Robert." In the WSCF archives for June 1940 is a whole set of such telegrams sent to and from Geneva, Bordeaux, Chambon-sur-Lignon and London. In view of the rapid advance of the German army in May 1940 and a possible invasion of Switzerland it was decided that the WSCF general secretary should work out of an office in Great Britain. The Mackie family was to travel by train to Bordeaux and from there to London, but they left a few days too late. Caught in the chaotic stream of refugees and defeated French soldiers they could not proceed beyond a village near Vichy. There some local people helped them to hide while the German army passed through. Later they managed to return to Switzerland, but only to leave again by car through southern France and Spain to Lisbon where they hoped to find a passage to North America, to open a WSCF office in Toronto, Canada. Suzanne wrote to Francis House: "I need not tell you how thankful we are to have Robert back here and to be able to talk things over with him again. I am so relieved that the experience of his trip was not too bad, but Robert is the type of man who would win every heart everywhere and would convert the devil himself to better feelings if the devil could be converted." The letter continues with news about people in France, eastern Europe and

Germany. A day after the Mackies left again Suzanne assured House that for the Federation's sake she was glad they were going to Canada: "For us who remain here it is hard because our sense of isolation grows from week to week. Robert's amazing gift of understanding and sympathy has helped me as nothing else could have."

Mackie and Suzanne met again only in 1945. But they kept in touch. Much of their correspondence must have been lost or never passed the censor. Over 150 letters, some of them as long as ten pages, have been kept, a strange dialogue in letters, exchanging financial and administrative information between the two WSCF offices and news of students in need, sharing thoughts and plans on present and future policies, encouraging each other in their isolation.

During the five years of his "exile" in North America, Mackie was constantly on the move. He visited university campuses in the USA and Canada, sharing information which he had received from Suzanne about European students, organizing and raising funds for student relief, securing American scholarships for Polish, Czech and Spanish students who had been stranded in France, and helping with pastoral work among prisoners of war in Canada. Twice he went on long visits to South America and once to Mexico. Suzanne briefed him: "Now about South America: the most rewarding work is with people, and this is just the kind of thing you will know how to do. A few hours spent with a young leader is far more valuable than platform speeches. The way to reach them is through friendship." When not travelling Mackie and his wife Dorothy edited the quarterly *The Student World* and the monthly *Federation News Sheet* which carried news and information received from Suzanne and others. From Geneva Suzanne managed to smuggle out key articles of the quarterly into Germany and the occupied countries. She also published adapted versions of the *News Sheet* in French and occasionally in two different German editions, one for neutral countries and another for Germany. In Toronto Morton became Mackie's associate and Mackie was thus able in the winter of 1942-43 to go to Great Britain and Sweden for three months, to make plans for the post-war period. On the World Day of Prayer in February 1943 he addressed a message to the students from London through the BBC and Suzanne listened to it in Geneva. In September 1943 the Swedish contact person, Rodhe, was able to go to Switzerland for meetings. By correspondence, such visits, and in other ways, communication within the network was maintained.

In the summer of 1940 Suzanne went through a period of deep depression following the collapse of the French army and the compromises the Vichy government made with Nazi Germany. "I do not have the strength any more even to get angry," she wrote to Bidgrain. Earlier her nationalism had been strong; she felt France was now fighting for Czechoslovakia and Poland, and she wrote: "How thankful and proud one is to be French! The duty to fight is so clear. The whole of European and Christian civilization is at stake." During the critical days of May 1940 Suzanne's hope was continuously nourished by prayer, and once she had "a strange experience": it was as if the whole country was suddenly lifted in prayer. "And the conviction was given me that God would save us; only He can overcome the demonic powers of destruction now raging through the world. And He will. How and when, I don't know. At least, this was the faith which came to me that day. Sometimes it wavers, and I feel as if we were going to live the days described in Revelation 13. These are really apocalyptic days. May God keep us faithful to the last, whatever comes."[5]

A month later national pride turned to national shame. Only prayer remained, prayer and resistance. When in November 1940 Suzanne heard that the national federation of girl scout movements in France had agreed to restrict the percentage of Jews and foreigners in its ranks, she resigned from her position as a vice-moderator. This created a stir, but she withdrew her resignation only when she got the assurance that this policy had been changed. In September 1941 Suzanne was one of a small group of French Protestant lay people and pastors, mainly past members of the Fédé, who gathered at Pomeyrol near Arles in southern France where a small French Protestant women's community received them. They issued the eight "theses of Pomeyrol". Visser 't Hooft was with them at the meeting, and he told them how other churches in Europe were taking a stand against national socialism. The theses were clearly patterned after the famous Barmen declaration of May 1934 by the Confessing Church in Germany. After summing up in six theses the truth of the gospel and the biblical testimony about church-state relationships, the seventh thesis declares: "The church protests solemnly against any legislation which excludes the Jews from human communities." The last thesis calls for resistance: "While accepting the material consequences of defeat, the church considers that resistance against every totalitarian and idolatrous influence is a spiritual necessity."[6]

Suzanne's main contribution to this resistance was her work in biblical training. From the 1914-18 war she knew how much both soldiers and prisoners needed information and spiritual nurture. Therefore she now began to send issues of the ecumenical press service and the sermons of Martin Niemöller of the German Confessing Church to key people. She produced her own literature for those who were in the army or in prison. Her faithful helper in the WSCF office, Adeline du Pasquier, wrote: "Suzanne is hard at work and produces more Bible studies, outlines and plans than I am able to type." Suzanne could still travel in the "free zone" of France and she used this opportunity to the full. "I cannot live long without some direct contact with human beings, and Bible study seems so much along the line of what I can contribute in the present situation," she wrote to Mackie, apologizing for her frequent absences from the Geneva office. In 1940-42 she frequently went to France for committee meetings of the Fédé, CIMADE and the French Protestant Youth Council. She led them in Bible study courses in Pomeyrol and at Les Grangettes in the Savoy mountains above Albertville. Then all frontiers were closed because in September 1942 the "free zone" was also occupied. Suzanne now often visited Swiss SCMs and she led several Bible seminars in Grandchamp near Neuchâtel, at another Protestant religious community of women, to which she became greatly attached. Together with Visser 't Hooft and the Swiss SCM, she organized ecumenical study weeks in 1943 and 1944.

The ministry of writing

With the closing of the frontiers Suzanne must have felt like the apostle Paul in prison. No wonder that the first biblical commentary she wrote was on Paul's letter from prison to a church under the cross, that of the Philippians. As with her other similar publications, Suzanne did not sit down to write a book. She simply noted down what gradually matured in private study and meditation and what was being tested in group Bible study. First, there was in 1940 a series of study outlines on Philippians published for soldiers on the front. This led to two weeks of Bible study in Pomeyrol and Grandchamp in 1941 where Suzanne worked with different groups. Only then the manuscript was finalized for publication: *L'épître aux Philippiens* (Lyons, 1942).

During the early years of the war, Suzanne gave a great deal of thought to the meaning of the cross and the message of the prophets. She decided to work on a French edition of her Spanish meditations on the cross, because she was convinced that the message of the cross was the only hope for a shattered world. In 1941 she wrote for prisoners of war in Germany eight meditations for the passion and Easter, and for soldiers on the front meditations on the seven words of the cross. Jeremiah had spoken strongly to the campers in Nunspeet just three weeks before the war. Suzanne therefore made a study outline on Jeremiah and expanded her Nunspeet lectures for a French edition. Another prophetic book began to fascinate her, and in May 1943 she wrote to Mackie: "Except for newspapers (they are really worth reading these days) I have been living in the sole company of Isaiah for nearly three weeks. And very stimulating company it is, I can assure you." At a Bible study course in Grandchamp she attempted to give the substance of the 66 chapters of the Book of Isaiah in six talks. Suzanne read aloud long passages of a new translation of the prophecies with only a minimum of introductory and explanatory comments. The prophetic voice and the poetry were given priority over the interpreter's reflections. The ancient biblical texts became oral tradition once again, and spoke to people in the world of 1943 A.D. as they did in the 8th century B.C. to the people in besieged Jerusalem and to the Jews of the 7th and 6th centuries B.C.

As Suzanne could no longer travel outside Switzerland, writing became her way of helping friends in the network. The first project took a long time to complete: a Bible study handbook, commissioned in 1937. Like many others with a passion for the Bible, Suzanne always wanted to let the biblical witnesses speak to people, rather than to write books about the Bible. Nevertheless, the drafts of the three-part handbook were gradually taking shape. Part I deals with why we should study the Bible, what the Bible is all about and what scientific approaches are used to explore its message. Part II is devoted to methods, reports on the result of an enquiry made in SCMs around the world, and makes suggestions on how a participatory way of Bible study can be prepared and animated and how a study group can function best. Part III gives examples of Bible studies on New Testament and Old Testament texts as well as on biblical subjects. The draft chapters were shared with the Mackies in Canada for critical comments. Each chapter was rewritten on the basis of suggestions made by them and by Visser 't Hooft. The final manuscript was sent back to Canada in January 1942 and four months later the book appeared there under the title *Rediscovering the Bible: Bible Study in the World Student Christian Federation* (Toronto, 1942). Nobody at that time suspected that a book written under such difficult circumstances would become a classic. Because of the war it had only a limited distribution, but within months a reprint had to be brought out. By 1943 Chinese and Swedish adaptations were published and in early 1944 a Spanish edition appeared. [7]

Suzanne had begun to make a French translation when Visser 't Hooft asked her to expand the manuscript, going beyond the experience gained in the WSCF and showing how the Bible had spoken to the confessing churches and how it could continue to speak to Christians in local parishes, sustaining them in their vocation in the world. The writing of this longer volume took much time and labour. It followed the same pattern as *Rediscovering*, but Suzanne added a substantial part on the Bible and the oikoumene. This rich summing up of what scholars and churches had learned about Bible study might not have been completed if the frontiers had been open between 1942 and 1945! *Le renouveau biblique: Principes, méthodes, applications pratiques* (Neuchâtel, 1945) appeared in the series "Ecclesia Militans", one of the first books to be published by the WCC in process of formation. Through its several editions and translations it became the main manual for biblical renewal in the post-war decade.

A second writing project was a WSCF history, planned to appear for the Federation's fiftieth anniversary in 1945, but it took much longer than expected. Not that Suzanne lacked interest in the subject. The war forced many people to reflect on the course and the end of history. Suzanne reviewed the growing literature on "history seen from beyond history". She even transcribed for Dorothy Mackie a strange old prophecy from Alsace which she had come across, that of the 7th century Frankish princess and seer Sainte Odile: it foretells a terrible war, that Germany will be the anti-Christ and gain victories on the earth and the seas and in the air, but will ultimately be defeated. "This may be superstition, but it really gave me courage," she wrote, and to Francis House she expressed similar apocalyptic feelings: "I feel the need for a living tension between active human thinking and planning and constant readiness for the unexpected to happen and blow up our ready-made plans... I often look at the terrific and tremendous page of history that God is writing with the expectancy and amazement of a child waiting for the end of the story."

The manuscript on the WSCF history was completed in 1947, and the book finally appeared in 1948: *Cinquante ans d'histoire: La Fédération universelle des associations chrétiennes d'étudiants* (Paris). It is a fascinating historical account in which Suzanne uses all her gifts of storytelling. (Forty-five years later the book was translated into English and published in a shortened version for the WSCF's hundredth anniversary: *Fifty Years of History*, Geneva, 1993.)

By far the most important book of the war period had matured in Suzanne's mind for so long that it fell like a ripe fruit from the tree, and she had only to pick it and write it up. In the autumn of 1941 Erica

Brucker, a French YWCA worker, visited Suzanne and told her about a ski camp for high-school girls and young women students which she was organizing at Christmas in the chalet of Les Grangettes in the French alps. Suzanne asked whether she could come along and conduct some Bible studies. Visser 't Hooft was angry when he heard of this. How could she go in the middle of winter to such an isolated place high up in the snow? But when Suzanne had made up her mind she would not easily change it. With sledges and hot water bottles transportation up and down the mountain would be no problem, she assured Visser 't Hooft. At that time Suzanne was working on the studies for a Bible week in Grandchamp, "God's plan of salvation through the whole Bible". She suggested this theme for the camp. Reporting later to Mackie she wrote that she took the group of fifty girls through the whole Bible in eight hours and they seemed to enjoy the trip. Each morning Suzanne gave a short introduction before the girls went skiing. In the late afternoon they read the assigned passages and in the evening bombarded her with questions. It was a new experience for the girls to see the whole Bible this way. Suzanne recalled: "This view of the whole responds to something. And this is how my book began."

To see the Bible as a whole was nothing new for Suzanne. Ever since she had discovered the prophets in the summer of 1916, she had been reading the New Testament in the light of Old Testament testimonies and the Old Testament in the light of the life, passion and resurrection of Jesus. She often worked with biblical scholars such as Wilhelm Vischer, Oscar Cullmann, Roland de Pury, Théo Preiss, Franz-J. Leenhardt, Eduard Schweizer and Pierre Bonnard, all of whom encouraged her to do what they — as Old or New Testament specialists — did not dare to: present the whole message of the Bible in its great diversity and essential unity. French students taking the course for "women's ministries" at Geneva university used to go to Suzanne's flat to help with the house-work. Suzanne gave them chocolates, but what they enjoyed even more was to listen to the new biblical discoveries she was making about the relationship between the Old and the New Testament.

Suzanne worked diligently through the whole Bible, searching for the thread which holds the whole together. In March 1942 she was, with Bonnard, at a study week in Grandchamp where again she conducted the participants "from paradise to the holy city". May and June of that year she spent at Les Grangettes, where she was main organizer for a six-week Bible training course for leaders of all the Protestant youth movements in France. When Suzanne came down from her "Bible mountain" she told a student meeting in Geneva about the experience. During the discussion period, a shy theological student stood up and announced: "Anybody who wants to do something like that in Switzerland, see me at the end of the session", a challenge which Visser 't Hooft and Suzanne readily took up. They contacted that student, Marie-Jeanne de Haller (two years later Suzanne's colleague and successor in the WSCF) and helped her and other Geneva students to organize the first French-Swiss Bible camp for the Protestant youth movements. The camp took place at Vaumarcus above Lake Neuchâtel and, again helped by Bonnard, Suzanne led a new group through the whole of the Bible.

Now the book was ready in Suzanne's mind. In between her various activities and other writing projects she put it down on paper. *Le dessein de Dieu: Itinéraires bibliques* (Neuchâtel, 1945) became her "best-seller". It has gone through 12 reprints and has been translated into 13 other languages (English ed. *God's Unfolding Purpose*, Philadelphia, 1960). It tells the great story of God's love for creation, the nations, the people of Israel and the church. Although written in a clear, non-technical style, it is not easy reading; it calls for close reflection and considerable acquaintance with the Book, the Bible.

From relief to reconstruction

In the war-time correspondence between Mackie and Suzanne there are not many letters that do not deal with student relief. Friendship needs to become tangible. The story of this work of solidarity within the WSCF network began in 1937 in China. The student departments of the Chinese YMCAs and YWCAs worked together with the secular International Student Service (ISS) to assist the large student population to migrate from the East coast, where the invading Japanese had destroyed the universities, to the interior of China. Students in North America joined this effort, and started the Far Eastern Student Service Fund. In 1940 a similar European Student Relief Fund was set up jointly by the ISS, the Roman Catholic student organization Pax Romana and the WSCF, to help the growing number of European students among the refugees and the war prisoners. This fund was administered out of the WSCF offices in Geneva and a distant cousin of Suzanne, André de Blonay, carried the main responsibility for it. In 1943 the Far Eastern and the European funds merged to become the World Student Relief. Another and much less formal institution in Geneva for coping with war-time emergencies was the ECCO (the Emergency Committee of Christian Organizations), under whose auspices the representatives of all ecumenical bodies in Geneva met regularly to share information received from their various constituencies around the world and plan corporate action. Suzanne represented the WSCF on this, and shared the plans with Mackie and her friends in France.

Relief soon proved far more complex than a simple matter of collecting money for providing food, clothes, books and scholarships to students who desperately needed them. Letters often got lost or were delayed, and that led to misunderstandings. Many questions came up which should really have been discussed face to face between people in Geneva and in North America. How, for instance, could they help occupied France without helping Hitler and breaking the blockage? How could one remain true to one's political convictions and at the same time work for ecumenical solidarity with students in enemy countries? In Geneva the WSCF worked increasingly with the not yet officially founded WCC where much creative thinking and a growing relief activity developed, while in North America its chief partners were still the YMCA and the YWCA. The war was not seen the same way from Geneva and from outside Europe, and this led to different policies of relief. Suzanne, and even more Visser 't Hooft, felt that this war was completely different from former ones and that the spiritual issues were clear: Nazism against democracy. Mackie did not agree. According to him different wars were being fought. He warned his colleagues in Geneva not "to identify the war with its European, or Middle Eastern, phase. Many of the deductions naturally made in Europe do not fit the Far East, or even the Russian front... The spiritual issues are very apparent, but there are imperial, commercial and racial issues also."

Many of these critical issues could finally be discussed face to face in the winter of 1942-43 when Elliott, who was much involved in student relief on the American side, was able to visit Geneva, and in 1943-44 when Mackie could consult with Europeans on his visit to Britain and Sweden. While Mackie envisaged a great extension of material aid in and through the WSCF network, Suzanne consistently emphasized the specific spiritual vocation of the Federation: "I think we should try to provide good people to serve in the various relief agencies... I foresee a tremendous ecumenical task of bringing together the Christian youth of our various countries, strengthening their work, helping them to stand on their feet again, and I am inclined to think that we shall have to concentrate on our spiritual and cultural task much more than after the last war because the relief problem will be on such a scale that only major official organizations will be able to deal with it."[8]

In a lecture at a training course for workers of the European Student Relief Fund in 1944 Suzanne spoke on "The Moral and Spiritual Factors in Student Relief". She showed how material aid is a sign of the more fundamental dimension of student relief, namely that of friendship and of welcoming solidarity. She also insisted on the great task of "de-toxification" which would be needed after the war. People had been nourished for years on certain collective myths. The harmful effect of this would continue even after the myths had collapsed. The *human* in every human being must therefore be allowed time and opportunity to recover its character, to clear itself of poison. According to Suzanne, this healing process could best be fostered by international organizations with a religious basis, because they had a common point of reference and had never broken off communications.[9]

Within the network of the WSCF communications indeed had never ceased and the main reflection and planning gradually shifted from relief to reconstruction. General committees and world conferences could not meet but the WSCF began to organize regional consultations on "Thinking Ahead as Christians". The first of these took place in 1942 at Poughkeepsie, NY, USA, and at Presinge near Geneva, Switzerland. They were followed by similar meetings in the following years in the USA, Britain, Switzerland, Sweden, India, China and the River Plate area of Argentina. Students from various nations who studied in these countries came together to discuss the messages from other "thinking ahead" consultations and they shared their own thinking with others through *The Student World*. Suzanne was involved in the translation and circulation of these messages, and she was a participant in the three Geneva area meetings of 1942-44. The message from the first Presinge consultation lists eight fundamental questions to be faced in post-war Europe: Christian ethics; the basis of law; the search for truth; the acceptance of judgment; the relationship between one's ecumenical and national calling; the discovery of blessing in human suffering; coping with the phenomenon of hatred; and the special relationship between the Jewish people and the Christian church. A major contribution which Suzanne made in relation to this analysis of needs was through her studies on the biblical basis of law.

During the final years of the war Suzanne spent much of her time in helping to set up homes of rest and recovery for students who came out of the horrors of fighting and concentration camps. The European Student Relief Fund rented a hotel at Combloux in the Savoy mountains which could accommodate up to 80 students. When in summer 1945 the committee of the Fund met there, Suzanne as the representative of the WSCF had to face the communist members of the ISS who dominated the debate. They were, for instance, against giving any help to German students. On the last day Suzanne had to speak about spiritual renaissance in the university. She clearly explained the Christian position, showing where Christians and Marxists could work together and where they differed. The Marxists appreciated her frank exposition but she did not win them over to extending help to German students. Meanwhile de Haller had joined the WSCF staff in Geneva and through its summer chalet programme the Federation could begin its own work of welcoming and giving spiritual support to students irrespective of their citizenship.

"Mon Paris"

In September 1944 Suzanne received permission to go to the Savoy, not only to inspect the hotel in Combloux but also to meet old friends, Westphal, Duflo and others. They felt like children on the first day of vacation, Suzanne wrote. They rented a boat and celebrated their reunion on the lake at Annecy.

At the end of September a visitor from Paris came to Geneva. Suzanne wrote to Mackie: "I had Madeleine Barot here for four or five days. She is a great story-teller and to hear her describe the six days fighting in Paris of which she has been an eye-witness was very thrilling... She has an unbreakable energy; she had appointments all day long and our conversations were between midnight and two or three o'clock a.m. Her work in concentration camps and 'centres d'accueil' has not diminished but expanded and she is carrying on her evangelistic work now, among others, among those who yesterday were bullying her clientele."

Ten days later a YMCA delivery truck came from Paris to fetch German Bibles for prisoners, and a place was available for the return journey. No more appropriate vehicle could have been found for Suzanne. Her report about that visit in October-November 1944 recounts meetings with the French Protestant Youth Council, the Fédé and CIMADE, and contains news about student relief in France and the partly destroyed conference centre at Bièvres. Suzanne was greatly pleased to be able to guide the driver through her old city in the black-out. "With what unspeakable thankfulness, during the following days and weeks, I saw the old buildings one after the other, still standing, still beautiful." Suzanne also met many old friends, besides Barot, with whom she stayed: Maury, Bidgrain, Zander, Dumas, even Sarah Watson, still helping to run the international foyer in the Latin quarter. What impressed her most was the work begun by Jean

Bosc through the Protestant professional associations: groups of business-men, medical doctors, educators and social workers were meeting to explore what it meant to be a Christian in their professions.

Six months later, in May 1945, Suzanne was again in her beloved Paris, this time taking an old car of the European Student Relief Fund, driven by Yngve Frykholm, a Swedish relief worker. She wrote to Mackie: "Having got my permanent visa I could not resist the temptation of a short visit to France and had the luck to reach Paris on the evening of V-day. It was really a great thing to drive through France on the 8th of May, all the little villages were covered with flags, the church bells were tolling everywhere. At 10 o'clock at night we drove to the Arc de Triomphe flooded with light and tried to drive down the Champs Elysées. Of course after ten yards we got stuck in the crowd; a laughing youthful crowd jumped on every car or truck available... I wondered if the old Fund car would resist this treatment but it did and Yngve is such a poised and calm chauffeur that he simply went out and enjoyed the sight. The worst moment was when we tried to move again and the starter did not function, but a kind American pushed us forward and we finally got out of the stream by the next little side street. To finish the story of the car, Yngve had to make up his mind the next day to pay a new motor which works splendidly. But we drove down from Paris to Lyons at the rate of forty kilometers an hour, the most slow and peaceful drive I ever had." [10]

NOTES

[1] See *The Student World*, 1939-45, the editors' travel diaries of R.C. Mackie and the travel reports of R. Elliot, M.-J. de Haller, F. and M. House, Kiang Wen Han, T.C. Koo, H. Morton, B. Rodhe and L. Tucker.

[2] SdD, letter of 28 August 1938 to Visser 't Hooft.

[3] Visser 't Hooft, "A Letter from the Chairman", *The Student World*, 1941, p.280, and *Memoirs*, pp.105-94.

[4] Nansie Blackie, *In Love and in Laughter: A Biography of Robert C. Mackie*, Edinburgh, 1995.

[5] SdD, letter of 19 May 1940 to Mackie.

[6] Georges Casalis, "Les thèses de Pomeyrol", *Etudes théologiques et religieuses*, 1984, pp.474-77.

[7] In the English-speaking world this book is better known in its abridged edition of the WCC Youth department entitled *Discovering the Bible: A Practical Handbook for Bible Study*, Madras, 1952.

[8] SdD, letter of 17 July 1942 to Mackie.

[9] SdD, "The Moral and Spiritual Factors in Student Relief", *The Student World*, 1945, p.52.

[10] SdD, letter of 1 June 1945 to Mackie.

10
Passing on the Vision

On a dark rainy day in the winter of 1945-46 Willem Visser 't Hooft and Robert Mackie made an exploratory trip in the Geneva area to find a place where the planned Ecumenical Institute could be located. They looked at several large houses which were for sale or rent, but they were not satisfied. Now they stood in the freezing rooms of a large mansion above the village of Céligny, some twenty kilometres from Geneva.

The Château de Bossey

It was beautifully situated, overlooking Lake Geneva and the Savoy Alps, with a huge lawn, a park of majestic trees and a narrow lane leading right down to the lake. The present château was built in 1720, but its history reaches back to the middle ages. All that remains of the earliest buildings is a tower. The land and buildings had belonged to the bishop of Geneva who gave them to the Cistercian monks of the abbey of Bonmont above Nyon. Attached to the medieval tower is a small stone building where the Cistercians had their wine press. This ecclesiastical past and the symbolism of the wine press did not escape Visser 't Hooft. The 18th-century mansion itself has an interesting history, and succeeding owners had made additions to the building: one constructed a small tower, another added, at right-angles to the château, a large "orangerie" for his collection of paintings.

The building was ill-equipped to become a training centre. They could put four to six beds in all the large rooms on the first and second floor, but that would not be a satisfactory arrangement in the long run. Once there had been a chapel at Bossey, but no longer. Food would have to be brought into the dining room of the main building from a kitchen in an old detached chalet close to the mansion. Everywhere there were pictures of Napoleon. The father of the last owner, Colonel Chenevière, had been a great fan of the French emperor, but young people from many nations were unlikely to share his enthusiasm, especially after the devastating war years they had lived through. But in spite of all this the two men decided that this was the place for the institute.

For once money was not a problem, at least for the time being. In May 1945 Visser 't Hooft had been in New York. What he told friends over coffee after a private supper obviously made a great impression on John D. Rockefeller who was one of the guests. The following day Visser 't Hooft received an invitation to go and see the Baptist multi-millionnaire. "It soon became quite clear", he recalled in his *Memoirs*, that Rockefeller "was especially interested in the plan to create an ecumenical institute which would confront young people who had to rebuild their lives after years in the armies or resistance movements with the challenge of renewal in the life of the churches and the nations." Rockefeller was pleased with the plan presented but not with the proposed budget. "You have not asked for enough money," he told Visser 't Hooft. The cheque which the friends of the WCC finally received in November 1945 was for one million dollars, and the donor suggested that half of it be used for starting an ecumenical institute. With this money a beginning could be made in 1946. The following year a five-year lease of the Château de Bossey was arranged, a small working budget provided and the nearby large house of Petit Bossey was bought. Thus the stage was set for Suzanne's life and work for the next eight years — though she herself had no idea of what was happening.

A movement begins

During the war years Suzanne had had to remain in Switzerland. Now she was free to travel, and she did not want to be tied down to a specific place. During the winter of 1945-46 she had to finish the manuscript on the WSCF history. As there was now a vigorous young team of WSCF secretaries she was able gradually to free herself from headquarters responsibilities. Both Mackie and she had decided to resign from the youth and student ministry at the forthcoming general committee of the WSCF which was the first group to meet, or rather to "camp", at the Château de Bossey in August 1946. For spring and summer 1946 Suzanne's programme was already crowded; she had to be at a number of meetings in France. Her doctor had warned her that she was overworking and should slow down, but that did not prevent her from making plans for the future.

Ever since she had heard about the work Jean Bosc had started through the Protestant professional associations she had been thinking of the two different vocations Christoph Dieterlen and Tommy Fallot had chosen to follow. Of course it was too late now for her to become an engineer and attempt to serve as a Christian in a secular profession. But could she not at least help people in secular professions to think through the ethical implications of the Christian faith in the modern world? Through her Bible study work she had already begun to do so, but much more could be done. Persons working in the same profession or in different branches of the same business could be brought together to discern the will of God for them in their profession.

In the 1930s many people had rediscovered the reality and vocation of the church. The war experience then revealed to them the great gap between what they believed to be the calling of the church and what weak, unfaithful, self-centred establishments many churches had in actual fact become. On the front, in prisons and internment camps they had met committed secular humanists and convinced Marxists who had put them to shame by their readiness to die for what they believed in. Christians were being asked to give an account of the hope that they had, and only a few were able to do so in a convincing way.

Among them was Roland de Pury who had used his imprisonment by the Gestapo in Lyons for writing on scraps of paper a new type of biblical commentary in which the atmosphere of torture and the fears and hopes of a prisoner became the sounding board for the biblical text. [1] In another Gestapo prison in Berlin, Dietrich Bonhoeffer prayed and rethought the meaning of the Christian faith and the vocation of the church, and smuggled out of his cell letters and poems which became the most seminal Christian writing of the post-war period. [2] In Holland outstanding personalities of the resistance movement were confined to an internment camp; among them was Hendrik Kraemer who used that time of anxious waiting for helping to plan a thorough church renewal movement, reaching every single local congregation of the Dutch Reformed Church.

All those who thus struggled for a new vision made a similar discovery: the church would be able to fulfill its task only if it again became that people of God, that royal priesthood and holy nation, about which de Pury wrote when he was commenting on Peter's first epistle. In a world which had come of age, both in human betrayals and human potentialities, church members had to become mature Christians as Bonhoeffer so insistently wrote from prison. Christ's ministry would in the first place have to be carried on by the worshipping, witnessing and serving Christian congregations, through the ministry of the laity, as Kraemer went on reminding church leaders, pastors and priests, and lay people themselves. [3] Inspired by such an impetus the basic insights of the laity movement gradually reached far beyond Europe. Later they were summed up as follows: "The phrase 'the ministry of the laity' expresses the privilege of the whole church to share in Christ's ministry to the world... It is the laity who draw together work and worship; it is they who bridge the gulf between the church and the world, and it is they who manifest in word and action the lordship of Christ over that world which claims so much of their time and energy and labour. This, and not some new order or organization, is the ministry of the laity... The real battles of faith today are being fought in factories, shops, offices and farms, in political parties and government agencies, in countless homes, in the press, radio and television, in the relationship of nations. Very often it is said that the church should 'go into these spheres'; but the fact is that the church is already in these spheres in the person of its laity."[4]

This vision could be realized only if places and ministries were created to equip the laity for their twofold task of being present before God in worship as representatives of all human beings, and of being present as God's representatives in all the spheres of life as prophets of hope and priests of reconciliation. Many traditional church activities and church groups had become an end in themselves, diverting the laity from their true ministry of that double presence rather than equipping them for it. In 1945, in many countries of Europe lay training institutes and professional associations began to grow. In Holland the Church and World Institute in Driebergen, of which Kraemer had been one of the founders, started work. In Germany Helmut Thielicke and Eberhardt Muller became the pioneers of the first evangelical academy in Bad Boll. In Italy Waldensian young people began to build the agape centre under the leadership of Tullio Vinay. As soon as Reinhold von Thadden came out of Russian captivity he started the Kirchentag movement which spread from Germany to France and Scotland. In Scotland itself the Iona community had been helping lay people and pastors to be the church in and for the industrial society. Even before that, the British civil servant and great ecumenical statesman Joseph H. Oldham had become the inspiration for the Christian Frontier Movement and a forerunner of what was now being called the rediscovery of the laity. After the war Kathleen Bliss helped Oldham as the editor of *The Christian News Letter*. All these professional associations, lay centres, communities and publications were only the first-fruit of a worldwide movement, a groundswell in modern church history, for which Bossey and the Laity department of the WCC were to serve as a coordinating centre.[5]

It was in early 1945 that Bliss made an interesting proposal to Suzanne through Mackie. She suggested that she and Suzanne join forces and together publish a bilingual European *News Letter*. Suzanne wrote back to say that she felt inclined to accept the proposal though she had some reservations. She discussed the matter with her friends in France. In September 1945 she wrote: "Pierre Maury whom I saw here last week believes that my main task in France next year might be to help in the building up of a strong laymen's movement with the post-Fédé as the nucleus. That is a condition if the famous *Christian News Letter* proposal is to materialize." In January 1946 Bosc wrote to Suzanne that he had discussed her plans about the newsletter with members of the French Protestant professional associations, and in their name he now invited her to take charge of this work as soon as she returned to France. Suzanne's future thus seemed settled, but it did not take into account Visser 't Hooft's plans.

The creation of an ecumenical institute could contribute richly to the growing movement to facilitate the ministry and training of the laity. The money and place for the institute had been found, and now they must find the right person as director. Visser 't Hooft knew who would be best for the job and he was greatly pleased when someone else suggested the same name: Hendrik Kraemer, the prophetic layman, then professor of comparative religions at Leiden university in Holland. Kraemer was approached and accepted the offer, but because of current commitments and serious health problems he could take up the new assignment only in January 1948. Meanwhile Henry-Louis Henriod, Suzanne's former colleague on the WSCF ecumenical commission, had been asked to live in the chalet close to the Château de Bossey and to take over as interim director and warden of the institute. But they had to find another person to start the actual training programme of Bossey and later to assist Kraemer as a lecturer. Once again Visser 't Hooft knew who the best person for this task would be and he called on Suzanne. Whatever her own plans were, she *must* go to Bossey. When Visser 't Hooft set his mind on something, he had to get it without delay.

The heart of Bossey

The Ecumenical Institute was officially opened on 5 October 1946, with Marc Boegner presiding. Visser 't Hooft spoke on the objectives and Kraemer delivered the inaugural address. His theme was "The Christian Church in the World Crisis". After the others had left, Suzanne and Henriod stayed on in the ill-equipped house with the 37 young lay people

Right: Suzanne with Sarah Chakko in Lucknow during her second visit to India, 1936-37 (Fonds SdD).

Centre: The leadership team of CIMADE, probably in the 1960s. Left to right: Paul Evdokimov, André Rouverand, Véronique Laufer, Suzanne, François de Seynes and Jacques Beaumont (Fonds SdD).

Below: Suzanne in conversation with Senegalese women in Dakar, 1967 (Fonds SdD).

The early team of the Ecumenical Institute at Bossey, 1948, with two of the speakers. Left to right: D. T. Niles, Henry-Louis Henriod, Oliver Tomkins, Hendrik Kraemer and Suzanne (WCC).

The first four general secretaries of the WSCF. Left to right: Robert Mackie, Willem Visser 't Hooft, Henry-Louis Henriod and John R. Mott.

Below: A WSCF consultation at Bossey in 1949. Robert Mackie is in the third row. Suzanne, Marie-Jeanne de Haller and Willem Visser 't Hooft are in the second row, and Leon Zander and K. H. Ting are first and third from the left in the front row (WSCF).

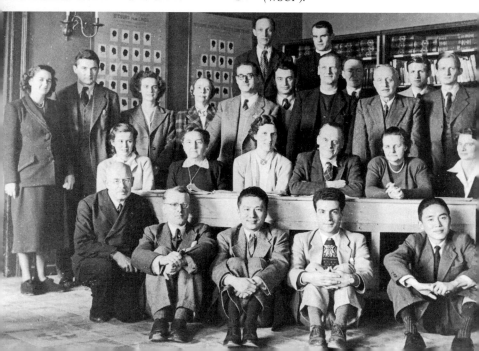

Right: Suzanne studying "Tintin", a comic strip, which friends had given her so she would be up to date with what young people were reading (Fonds SdD).

Centre: Suzanne in 1977 with Christoph Baker and his family (Fonds SdD).

Below: Suzanne was a passionate scrabble player even in her old age. Here she is playing with Lucette Pons in 1974 (I. Poznanski).

Following page: Suzanne at 80 in 1971 (P. Willi).

from 15 European nations who had come to participate in the first six-week course, most of them still under the shock of the war. There was no common language and there were no interpreters, only a programme which had been put together in haste. The roles of Henriod and Suzanne had not been clearly defined, which made their collaboration difficult. For the most part Henriod attended to the practical tasks and the welfare of participants while Suzanne dealt with the training programme where a good deal had to be improvized and she was very much on her own.

Perhaps the best way to give an idea of Suzanne's work during those early Bossey years is to describe a youth leaders' course in spring 1948 where I met her for the first time. Two longer lay courses and a few specialized conferences had already taken place. Kraemer was in the process of settling down to his work, but in 1948 he often had to travel for the Institute. As the national secretary of the Swiss SCM I had of course heard about the famous Miss de Diétrich. It was thus with considerable expectation that as a WSCF delegate I went to Bossey. The atmosphere of the château was more that of a youth work camp than of a solemn church meeting. An interpreter had been employed, but communication was still difficult, and volunteers from among the participants interpreted in the groups. How exciting it was for me in that post-war period to meet young people from all over Europe and famous leaders from far away — Asia, America and Africa!

Shortly after my arrival Suzanne called me to her office. When I entered the small room, cluttered with books and papers, I did not see her at first. She turned round from her desk, put her stiff, short legs to rest on her two walking sticks and looked up at me. She must have noticed my shock, but it did not seem to bother her. Nobody had told me that the great Suzanne de Diétrich was so small, almost dwarfish. She wanted to know everything about recent developments in the Swiss SCM. She told me that I was expected to be a group leader and that I had better be prepared for the following morning's session. This was her way of training people. So strong was her presence and so striking her personality that, like so many others who met Suzanne, I no longer noticed her physical disability by the time I left the office. I have forgotten the talks given by well-known lecturers during that course — on Christianity and Marxism, on the background and attitudes of young workers in industry, and on the ecumenical movement. I do not remember much of the Bible studies which Suzanne animated each morning during those three weeks, except the one on the message of the prophet Haggai. That spoke of the courage needed to address the task of reconstruction in a world of broken hopes, and it challenged us so strongly that we spent a whole night discussing and praying for our own broken hopes and communities.

As in many other early meetings at the Ecumenical Institute the youth leaders at that course were forced to face the enmities, hatreds and divisions created by the second world war. Participants from the Baltic states had come directly from camps for displaced persons. British, Dutch, Belgian, Hungarian, Czech and Greek participants were meeting Germans for the first time after the war. Some still suffered from the trauma of fighting on the eastern or western front. Others had been in prison camps or had lost loved ones in the battles and bombardments. Many still strongly felt the humiliations they had had to undergo in an occupied country. During the first week of the course we were polite to one another. In the second week the Germans were gradually isolated and few people spoke to them. Then came the explosion, heated accusations, and a total breakdown of communication and fellowship. A day of silent retreat led to mutual confession and forgiveness, and a service of holy communion. We had experienced something of what the ecumenical movement costs, and during the last days of the course we hesitantly began to reconstruct a new fellowship.

Where was Suzanne in all of this? An outside spectator would hardly have noticed her presence. As the leader of the course she took no initiatives to alleviate the situation. She let the participants struggle and suffer things through. But she was there in the midst of us. Until late into the night she sat in her office, ready to listen to everyone who went to her. Through the way she had helped the participants to discover God's action in the history of the people of Israel and by her pastoral presence in the group, she introduced a new dimension into the breaking and then the healing fellowship. She was so much the heart of the whole course that none of us suspected how often she was unhappy and lonely during these early years in Bossey.

The change from the atmosphere of informal team work in the WSCF to a more official and ecclesiastical one proved more difficult for Suzanne than had been anticipated. True, Visser 't Hooft helped her in making the first contacts with speakers, but after that she was left alone with the follow-up and all the crises that arose. She appreciated the presence at Bossey, for several months, of S.S. Selvaretnam of the Christa Seva Ashram in Sri Lanka. Young colleagues from the WCC, among them Paul Abrecht and J.C. Hoekendijk, came to help with some of the courses and conferences, but few of her colleagues working in Geneva and travelling around the world fully understood the pressures involved in staying put at Bossey for months and being continually open to the members of ever-changing groups. Suzanne also felt that Mackie, who had become the director of the WCC programme for interchurch aid and service to refugees, was growing away from her. This was not true, but extending the initially Europe-centred work into a worldwide relief and reconstruction programme kept him totally busy. During the first 15 months Suzanne's living quarters in the château were far from ideal. She had her small office on the ground floor where she spent up to 18 hours a day, and a bedroom on the second floor from which she came down with her sticks over slippery staircases in the morning and to which she returned late at night. Suzanne often wondered whether the location of the Institute was the right one. According to her the château was "too luxurious and not very welcoming". She confessed that for a long time she did not feel at home there. She would have preferred a mobile team with a modest home base rather than a large conference centre in the idyllic Swiss countryside.[6]

Nevertheless, gradually she learned to love the château and the exciting work of the Institute. It became so much her home that later she often returned to Bossey. With a second gift from John D. Rockefeller the château could be bought and in 1951-52 the whole place was substantially redesigned. Many smaller rooms and a dormitory were installed so that up to eighty persons could now be accommodated. The old chalet was replaced by a multi-purpose building. The château and the "orangerie" were linked together, providing an entrance hall. A proper kitchen, a better-equipped lecture room, an office and a small library were added, and the former wine press at the bottom of the medieval tower was transformed into a chapel. Suzanne saw to it that the architect took note of the fact that believers of all Christian confessions were to worship there and that, for example, the place of the altar was theologically significant. The interpreter, Ilse Friedeberg, was a remarkable person; she would sometimes take notes while simultaneously interpreting, and later explain to students what the speakers were really trying to say. She especially helped Orthodox participants to find their place in a still predominantly Protestant milieu. From late 1948 Simone Mathil took over most of the administrative work. After the renovations Renée Sturm became the hostess and introduced into the life of Bossey "the blue angels", young volunteers from many countries who helped — and still help — with the household chores.

There were romantic elements in the history of the château which much amused Suzanne. At the beginning of the 19th century the French

Protestant writer, Baroness Germaine de Staël-Necker, during her exile in Switzerland, had lively discussions with European intellectuals and artists in her salons at the Château de Coppet. Now, a few kilometers from Coppet, another French baroness, Suzanne de Diétrich, did the same thing, though with a rather different Protestant theology and towards a different goal. In 1808 Madame de Staël bought the Château de Bossey for her son Auguste who promptly sold it two years later. Auguste de Staël was later active in revival groups in Paris and helped to create evangelistic societies, just as some of Suzanne's spiritual ancestors had done.

As with every true château, Bossey has its share of ghost lore. Suzanne liked to tell the story of Elisabeth Lange, a former owner of Bossey. She was a beautiful actress from Paris, married to a rich Belgian ship-owner who bought the château for her in 1817. "La bonne châtelaine de Bossey", as she was called, died in 1825 while undergoing treatment in Italy. Her husband could not live without her, and he had her embalmed body brought to Bossey in a coffin with a glass lid. For over a year he kept it in one of the salons of the château. Then the police ordered him to bury the body, but one night he took the coffin to the Catholic church in Carouge just outside Geneva. There ends the story... but not quite. Since that time strange things happen and strange noises are heard on the second floor. Suzanne once told a group half-jokingly that she flatly refused to move into a room upstairs that was offered to her!

Two events made Suzanne's life in Bossey much happier than during the difficult first years. In 1950 she bought a small car adapted to her handicap. She took driving lessons from the chauffeur of the Institute and became mobile. Many participants of courses were invited for often nerve-racking outings in the Swiss and French Jura mountains. She also acquired a faithful companion, a small dog called Choucky, and they understood each other very well. Once, when the dog of a lonely Russian refugee died and the man covered the dog's grave with many flowers, she wrote: "I am sure that in the Orthodox world there are transfigured dogs, and I do not dislike the thought."

The Kraemer-Suzanne team

What fundamentally changed Suzanne's initial hesitations about Bossey was her deep respect for Hendrik Kraemer with whom an excellent collaboration and growing friendship developed.

In a report on the the first three years Suzanne lists 12 courses with about 450 participants from 45 countries, mainly from Europe, with a slowly growing number from the Americas, Asia, the Middle East and Africa. They came from 15 Christian denominations, predominantly Protestant, with a small but increasing number of Orthodox and Catholics. These three- to eleven-week courses were in the first place planned for lay people and youth leaders, though later courses for theological students, pastors and missionaries became regular events. During the first three years there were 13 shorter and more specialized conferences with about 340 participants. Four of these became annual events: those for directors of lay institutes and groups, people working in industry, teachers and medical professionals. There were also conferences for other professions, e.g. journalists and political leaders, and on specific themes, such as "the Christian doctrine of work", "the church and the Jewish people" and the "meaning of history" with university professors from different faculties. For 1950 conferences were planned on family problems, the foundations of international law, the challenge of modern biology for biologists and theologians, the arts, social work, and the sociological approach in the strategy of the church where sociologists and theologians critically evaluated the theme.

A gradual change in emphasis will be noticed. The first official report of the Institute, prepared for the inaugural assembly of the WCC in the summer of 1948 in Amsterdam, indicates that "the experiences of the first two years have led the board to modify the original plan to some extent" by adding to the general courses specialized meetings such as those mentioned above, often called the "frontier conferences". After the renovations in Bossey, there was another shift of emphasis. From October 1952 an annual four-and-a-half-month Graduate School of Ecumenical Studies was conducted in collaboration with the theological faculty of the University of Geneva.[7] The accent thus shifted to more theologically trained participants, and besides the ongoing specialized conferences the main summer courses were for pastors, missionaries and theological students.

What remained unchanged was the central place given to group Bible study, animated mainly by Suzanne, but often led also by Kraemer. The daily rhythm of worship too continued: morning prayer, led by participants, a regular period of intercession at noon, led by the Institute staff, and evening prayers at the close of the day. Many meetings included also a period of silent retreat in preparation for a holy communion service.

One wonders how the small staff could cope with all this. Suzanne certainly could not slow down as her doctor had advised. The staff invited the best people in the various fields, but these scientists, philosophers, politicians and theologians had to be found, persuaded to come to Bossey without honoraria, and briefed about the special transcultural and inter-confessional groups gathering at the Institute. Not only speakers and resource persons but also qualified participants had to be found, which often involved much work in small preparatory committees and extensive correspondence.

Suzanne carried the major responsibility for the courses, the Bible studies and much of the liturgical life. She assisted Kraemer in many of the conferences, especially those with educators, lawyers and people from industry. Initiating the annual conferences for directors of lay institutes and groups, she could now extend to a universal scale what in 1945 she had intended to do in France. It was this group gathering at Bossey that insisted that the WCC appoint a secretary for laity concerns. From the end of 1949 Hans-Hermann Walz, the study secretary of the evangelical academy of Bad Boll, served in this position and spent more than half his time working at the Ecumenical Institute. Reporting about the first conference with lay institute directors Suzanne enthusiastically wrote to Visser 't Hooft: "They are bubbling with ideas and projects and we missed you here. What a pleasure to work with a group of intelligent men!"

Suzanne was indeed better at working with men than with women. Not that she neglected the role of women. She was all along committed to women's participation in civic life and had been much involved in the first international conference for women students, organized in 1933 by the WSCF in Simonshof, Austria. But both her biblical studies and her personal experience confirmed her in the conviction that, with their own special gifts and intelligence, women could best serve in collaboration with men, complementing and humanizing the special masculine gifts. As early as 1936 she had explored and defended this view in an article on "Paradise Lost". [8] Although there is too much sexual stereotyping in that article, it is still worth reading. Such stimulating collaboration could in fact happen on the board of Bossey. Von Thadden, Mackie and Visser 't Hooft were its chairman, vice-chairman and secretary; among the board members were men like Jean Bosc, Paul Evdokimov, Martin Niemöller, D.T. Niles and Denis de Rougemont, and women like Madeleine Barot and Kathleen Bliss.

Most outstanding in this group was the man who really shaped Bossey, Hendrik Kraemer. Many know him only as the author of the famous study book for the international missionary conference in Tambaram in 1938, *The Christian Message in a Non-Christian World*. He is often seen as the one who fought against syncretism, the mixing of different religious beliefs, and as the one who became the spokesman for Karl Barth's "no" to any facile dialogue with people of other faiths. In fact Kraemer's thinking was much less influenced by Barthian theology than by Blaise Pascal and a continual going back to what he called "biblical realism". In this Suzanne and he immediately recognized each other as kindred spirits. Kraemer was a far greater scholar than Suzanne. Around his desk in his large office at Petit Bossey there were always several piles of books, which changed according to the conference he was preparing for: here the latest publications on psychology, there studies on biology, then another pile of linguistic treatises, writings on Islamic mysticism, and always a pile of novels from different cultures. Kraemer suffered from insomnia, and through the long nights read books on every conceivable field of human knowledge — if he was not involved in passionate conversations with a secular humanist, a Muslim thinker or a young student who questioned the church and the Christian faith. Suzanne wrote about him: "He always seems to have read everything important... It is this passionate interest in all human thought worthy of the name which enables him to engage in true dialogue with the world. He knows that all authentic communication between human beings requires a double intelligence, of the head and of the heart. He knows how to read, but also how to listen."[9]

There were many factors that informed their partnership. Both of them abhorred ecclesiastical politics. As lay people both were keenly interested in theology but had a healthy suspicion of theological speculations that were not closely related to the struggles of faith in this world and time. Both were extremely demanding, but they were also ready to give time for leisurely pastoral conversations with young people who needed their help. What ultimately mattered most to both were the realities of this world and history, seen, challenged and acted upon from the perspective of another, more lasting reality which they liked to describe in the words of Pascal: "God! The God of Abraham, Isaac and Jacob! The God of Jesus Christ! *Not* the God of the philosophers and the scholars."

An ecumenical laboratory

"Bossey is a sort of laboratory where ecumenism is being lived," Suzanne once wrote. Ecumenism meant for her not simply a joyful coming together to know one another across confessional and cultural boundaries, but also to suffer together in the common search for truth.

Many have indeed suffered at Bossey as their spiritual and cultural presuppositions were suddenly called in question by co-participants. Some lost their faith. Many more were tested in their faith and thus came out of this laboratory strengthened and deeply enriched. Before the war the WSCF and other youth movements were the training ground for future ecumenical leaders. Now Bossey began to play a similar role, especially through its graduate school. Thousands of people in all continents received there a new vision of the church's vocation in the world.

However, Bossey can also become an artificial place, outside the real world. In March 1968 Suzanne spoke to the Bossey staff about the early years of the Institute. She had come directly from a Paris in the throes of unrest. At CIMADE she had been in daily contact with Latin American, African and French students. No wonder that on that occasion she expressed again some of the misgivings she had had in the late 1940s about the location of the Ecumenical Institute in the peaceful Swiss countryside.

Only a few of Suzanne's personal letters from her eight years at Bossey have been preserved, and one gets the impression that, despite her growing love for the place and her commitment to its work, she was not really happy there. Travelling was in her blood and she could not easily reconcile herself to being tied down to a task which allowed her little freedom of movement. She had prepared the Bible study outlines for the second world conference of Christian youth, in July 1947 in Oslo, but she could not attend the conference. With Kraemer she was in the preparatory group for the WCC Amsterdam assembly's second section on "The Church's Witness to God's Design". During the assembly itself she served as a consultant for the committee on "The Significance of the Laity in the Church" for which Kraemer acted as secretary, and until 1954 as chairman of the WCC layman's committee. In July 1949 she helped Walz and Kraemer to organize the European laymen's conference in Bad Boll: she prepared, introduced and concluded the daily Bible studies on texts from the Book of Acts, and Walz reported that for many of the 220 lay participants this was the most valuable part of the whole meeting.

Though Suzanne did not like such large meetings it was in this border area of Bible study and the ministry of the laity that she felt most at home. That was why she also helped with the preparation of the laity section of the 1954 assembly of the WCC in Evanston, USA, although she herself did not go. Through such work, coming out of the experience of Bossey but done in the wider WCC context, the Institute became in the true sense of the word a "seminary", "a place of sowing", as Kraemer once said in a director's report. From 1950 onwards such sowing also happened annually, in the Bossey courses at Berlin, especially organized for people from East Germany and occasionally other eastern European participants who, for political reasons, could not come to Bossey. Suzanne liked to participate in these. During the transformations of the château in 1951-52 her dream of a mobile training team became a reality at least partially, for Bossey courses were then held in the French centre of Bièvres, the Swiss centre of Gwatt and the Dutch centre of Woudschoten.

A lecture tour in the USA in early 1952 brought Kraemer into contact with the Episcopalian lay centre of Parishfield near Detroit, and for several years there was an intimate working relationship between Bossey and Parishfield. Kraemer rightly guessed that the Parishfield community with its great simplicity of life and its contacts with the industrial world of Detroit was a place that would appeal to Suzanne and in 1953 he sent her to work with that community for several months. Parishfield did in fact become Suzanne's USA home during her frequent stays in North America in the following decades.

NOTES

[1] Roland de Pury, *Pierres vivantes: Commentaire de la première épître de Pierre*, Neuchâtel/Paris, 1944.

[2] Dietrich Bonhoeffer, *Letters and Papers from Prison*, London, 1953.

[3] Hendrik Kraemer, *A Theology of the Laity*, London, 1958.

[4] *The Evanston Report: The Second Assembly of the World Council of Churches, 1954*, report on section VI on "The Laity: The Christian in His Vocation", London, 1955, pp.161,168. For a historical survey of the laity movement see S.C. Neill & H.R. Weber, eds, *The Layman in Christian History*, Philadelphia, 1963.

[5] Information about such centres and lay movements is to be found in the WCC periodicals *Laymen's Work* (1951-55) and *Laity* (1956-68) and the publications of the WCC Laity department, *Signs of Renewal: The Life of the Lay Institute in Europe*, Geneva, 1956; *Centres of Renewal*, Geneva, 1964; *Meet the Church: The Growth of the Kirchentag Idea in Europe*, Geneva, 1959. On brother- and sisterhoods see Lydia Praeger, ed., *Frei für Gott und die Menschen: Das Buch der Bruder- und Schwesternschaften*, Stuttgart, 1959.

[6] SdD, multicopied *Mémoire sur l'avenir de Bossey*, 25 August 1949.

[7] Cf. the special issue of *The Ecumenical Review* on the Graduate School of Ecumenical Studies, 1961-62, pp.1-81.

[8] SdD, "Paradise Lost", *The Student World*, 1936, pp.204-207.

[9] SdD, "Kraemer et l'œcumene", *De Heerbaan*, 1958, pp.108f., 111.

11
An Active Retirement

November 1954. Retirement age for women in the World Council of Churches was 63: Suzanne should have retired nine months back. Now it was time to leave Bossey and professional ecumenical service.

Would she settle down to a quiet retirement? That, predictably, did not happen. For her birthday in January 1961 W.A. Visser 't Hooft wrote: "Is it really true that you are 70 years old? I can't believe it. Ladies of seventy don't do what you do.... My hope is that you will be able to help the ecumenical movement for many more years, just as you have done through the preparation of the brochure for New Delhi which is being used in parishes all over the world."

The brochure was the booklet *Jesus Christ: The Light of the World* (the theme of the third WCC assembly which met at the end of 1961), a study guide for local parishes which had appeared in more than thirty languages. Although Suzanne declined the invitation to participate at the assembly she had helped to prepare the booklet, which included eight Bible study outlines on texts from Genesis to Revelation.

What was so extraordinary about what Suzanne was doing? In spite of her physical handicap, now steadily getting worse, she travelled frequently, in Europe, North America, Latin America. At 74, she was to go on a long teaching tour in Africa. More astonishing still was her continuing openness to new ideas, her readiness to listen, learn and start all over again if former ways of teaching and writing proved to be dated or inadequate for the new time and cultural environment.

The search for a home

Where was to be Suzanne's home, both geographically and spiritually, after Bossey? She could have joined one of the religious communities, Pomeyrol in southern France or Grandchamp near Neuchâtel, Switzerland. Both Antoinette Butte and Geneviève Micheli, the founding mothers of these two communities, were her friends. When she left Bossey in November 1954 she did go for a few weeks to Grandchamp where she shared an apartment with Renée Sturm, who had been hostess at the Ecumenical Institute and had left Bossey about the same time as Suzanne. But life as a sister in a religious community was not what she really wanted.

Should she return to the forests of northern Alsace which she loved so much? Every year she used to go back to the area, and usually stayed with her cousin's family in the "Moulin", near Niederbronn, where she was born. But all her sisters had died and none of their children lived in Alsace. Suzanne had a strong sense of family, so should she not spend the rest of her life close to one of her nephews or nieces?

Her links with the family of her oldest sister, Mary von Türcke-de Dietrich in Germany, were not strong. She continued to respond in writing and financial support to requests which came from Mary's descendants. The unmarried Marguerite de Dietrich had joined her younger sister Amélie Trew in Western Canada, where she had died in 1952. Suzanne's youngest sister, Adèle Pfalzgraf, took her own life in 1933. She did keep in touch with that family but her closest contacts by far were with a son and a daughter of Amélie; Bicky and Jo were like her own children. Jo had a similar physical handicap, which made the link between aunt and niece even stronger. Suzanne invited her several times to Bossey and made it possible for her to participate in the second world conference of Christian youth in Oslo. It was during that conference in 1947 that Jo's mother died in Vancouver. Some months later news reached Bossey that just before Christmas Jo had been seriously wounded in a car accident near Paris. Suzanne immediately went to Paris and visited Jo daily at the American hospital, where Jo met her future husband, Bob Tanner, an officer of the American army serving in Europe. They settled down in Sacramento, California, and eventually had two sons, Mike and Keith, who used to stay with Suzanne in Paris and for holidays in the mountains. Jo's brother Bicky was already married and worked for the forestry department of British Columbia. He was very close to Suzanne in her old age. On her teaching tours in North America she invariably visited her two "children", but she was too much of a European to emigrate to North America for her retirement.

In 1951-52 Suzanne had made plans to settle some time later near the Fédé conference centre of Bièvres. An agreement was drawn up with the French SCM, according to which she received a plot of land on the campus of Bièvres to build a house which would become the property of the Fédé after her death. Somehow the plan fell through; Suzanne may have had second thoughts about the location and the cost of building.

Finally she decided to buy an apartment in Paris in a block where CIMADE also planned to put up people. She could move in only in the spring of 1956. Many people from around the world stayed there during her absences overseas or as her guests when she was in Paris. Did Suzanne really feel at home there? In letters to a Finnish friend she wrote that she never quite found her place, not even in her flat in Paris. It was more than ecumenical restlessness. Her feeling of homelessness had a deeper dimension. When leaving WSCF service in 1946 she had felt called to a ministry in the structures of the world, alongside people in secular professions. During the student relief years she had worked together with secular humanists and Marxists who were rethinking the role of the university and concerned to bring about a responsible society in the secular world. Here, Suzanne thought, was an exploration she would love to be associated with.

The call to work at the Ecumenical Institute at Bossey, the collaboration with Hendrik Kraemer and the worldwide reflection on the ministry of the laity seemed at first to go in that direction. But the Bossey programme was then geared more to serve theological students, pastors and priests. In July 1950, Suzanne received a letter which must have taken her by surprise: at the proposal of Théo Preiss, the council of the Protestant theological faculty at Montpellier in France had decided to confer on her an honorary doctorate in theology. The convocation took place in the autumn of that year. After the list of students, cited for their academic excellence, had been presented, Dean Henri Leenhardt said that one name was missing: "It is not the name of a student — though when do we cease to be students? It is not the name of a pastor or a theological professor. It is a name revered for almost forty years by generations of young people and generations of less young people; the name of a woman of whom one can say that she is the greatest lay theologian of our time, Miss Suzanne de Diétrich." [1]

Almost against her will Suzanne was now a theologian. She did not take the dean's words too seriously, but the doctorate had unexpected consequences. B.R. Lacy, president of Union Theological Seminary in Richmond, USA, who had also received an honorary doctorate from Montpellier, invited her to become the first guest professor at his seminary. That marked the beginning of a long theological teaching career. People from all over the world who participated at Bossey Bible studies animated by Suzanne invited her for similar work in their countries and churches. Her books were now translated into many languages. This in turn created a demand for further literature in the field.

Suzanne thus became, in one sense, the "prisoner" of her past ministry, especially the "prisoner" of Bible study. She had hoped to become more involved as a Christian in the structures of the world, but she was now almost forced to remain involved as a theological teacher in the structures of the church. Neither in institutional church life nor in the secular world did she feel totally at home. Until the end of her life she was to remain a traveller and a pilgrim.

Biblical teacher in North America

The theological seminary in Richmond had some 200 undergraduate resident theological students, mainly southern Presbyterians, a group of advanced students doing graduate work, and an additional hundred women and men enrolled in the training college for lay workers opposite the seminary campus. During the three-month term in spring 1955 Suzanne had to teach a main three-hour course each week for this student body and offer some optional courses in the form of seminars for smaller groups. Somewhat intimidated by such a new task, Suzanne went to her Grandchamp retreat for some hard preparatory work. She could have chosen the subject of one or several of her former publications, but in the light of the church-world tension in her life she chose to explore further that aspect of the biblical message. Writing to Lacy she said: "I would like to give a course... somewhat on the lines of my booklet *Le dessein de Dieu*, but centred more definitely on the 'church-world' relationship... When we read the Bible our first impression is that it is all centred on the people of God. Then we become aware that, while this is true, the people of God are seen as an instrument for the salvation of the world. There is a constant tension between the fact of separation from the world and mission to the world. Thus the big danger threatening the people of God is on the one hand a ghetto-religion and on the other hand absorption in the surrounding civilization."[2]

Suzanne need not have worried about how her teaching in a theological college would be received. Both students and professors responded enthusiastically to her message and to the way she changed academic practices. Instead of sitting for an exam, students were asked to prepare a Bible study outline on a biblical image (e.g., the "vine", the "shepherd", the "body") which she then discussed with each student. She was given a standing invitation to come back to Richmond whenever she wanted.

Suzanne wrote to Tania Metzel, a church worker in French women's prisons whom she much admired, telling her about a visit she had made to an American women's prison and adding: "Out of the blue I have been made a professor of theology... The boys are very nice and take me very seriously... I must say, though, that I am heart and soul immersed in my work, with all that remains of my body, brain and heart... Week after week I have the astonishing experience of God's grace. He definitely likes to work with old broken vessels."

After completing her teaching term Suzanne spent some time with her family in the USA and Canada, and went to Parishfield to revise her lectures for publication. While there she broke her leg and was forced to rest. During the morning eucharist of the community, just before she had the accident, she had said a prayer which was not quite in her style: "Make me faithful in days of health and days of illness." Many people thought that she would never be able to *walk* out of the hospital at Ann Arbor in Michigan where she was taken. But four months of hospital treatment and a month of convalescence at Parishfield, and Suzanne's will to live made it possible for her to walk again. It was a time of much suffering, and of profound reflection on the Book of Job. It was also a time when she experienced much care and love from friends in Parishfield and from far away. Bicky drove five thousand kilometres from Vancouver Island to Ann Arbor and back just to see his aunt. A fruit of that prolonged stay in Michigan was the first major book Suzanne wrote in English, *The Witnessing Community*, based on the courses she had given in Richmond.

Suzanne was in North America on five more long visits (1957-58, 1959, 1961, 1963-64, 1966). She taught and spoke in very different settings: theological colleges, lay training centres (especially Parishfield and Montreat), large denominational conferences, interdenominational student assemblies, smaller clergy groups and many local parishes. She helped the southern Presbyterians to start a lay school of theology. Twice she worked for the Protestant Episcopal Church, giving clergy and lay training courses in several of its dioceses from the Atlantic to the Pacific ocean. For two months she was involved in a missionary training programme of the United Presbyterian Church. During the last visit, her main biblical teaching was for the American Baptist Church and focused on questions of justice and freedom. On all these visits Suzanne went back to Parishfield where she became a pastoral counsellor for many members and to the community as a whole.

Suzanne often recalled the week she spent in November 1953 with a local church at Little Rock, Arkansas, well-known in the American civil rights movement. The members of this congregation were mainly representatives of liberal professions, among them some thirty medical doctors. As a result of their courageous involvement in the civil rights movement, and guided by a wise pastor, this congregation had dropped all the busy church activities typical of American Protestantism. Only Sunday worship and participation in one of the 25 weekly groups for serious Bible study were maintained. Occasionally a biblical scholar was invited to help with an intensive week-long training for leaders. Members were thus equipped for their costly presence both in their vocations and in the struggles of their city. It was the kind of congregation Suzanne loved, and she enjoyed leading them through a series of studies on Colossians.

Suzanne continued to be critical of America, especially of American politics, but she also learned to appreciate the openness and the courage to experiment which she came across in many places. Despite her mistrust of the American fascination with methods she was ready to write typically American study booklets and to learn new ways of teaching, e.g. the use of role play in Bible study. "What makes me sad is to see the French always imprisoned within their frontiers, something I can't stand any longer... If you go to America, the fact that you are a foreigner, that you come from somewhere else, makes the people receive you all the more gladly, and they are happy to listen to you. They are open and have a kind of curiosity about what happens elsewhere, about the way people think in other places." [3]

Love affair with Latin America

Suzanne's love for Latin America, which began during her first visit to that continent in 1937, was revived when in 1959 she was invited to help with a student and youth leaders' Bible course for the whole continent, organized jointly by the WSCF and the WCC Youth department. It was held at Campos de Jordan, a vacation village in the Brazilian sierra, and was immediately followed by a more concentrated course for the Brazilian SCM. Her travel schedule included several other places in Brazil with lectures in theological seminaries and universities. Going south, Suzanne conducted a passion week retreat in Colonia Valdense, Uruguay, and worked with the United Evangelical Seminary in Buenos Aires and with the Lutherans in Argentina. In Chile she participated in a Pentecostal worship service in a slum area of Concepción which at once intrigued and challenged her. Further north again, in Peru, she led a Bible seminar for pastors and missionaries and spoke in the state university of San Marco, the oldest Latin American academic institution. This was followed by a course in Mexico City. Heading north again Suzanne was welcomed at Los Angeles by Jo and Bicky, and she had a period of rest before she embarked on another six-week programme of travel and teaching in the USA.

During her travels through Latin America Suzanne saw signs of renewal in the Roman Catholic Church. In Brazil she met Dominican fathers who told her about the founding of a Benedictine centre for biblical studies. In Chile two Jesuit professors invited her to lecture at the Catholic university. She could not accept their invitation because of her tight schedule, but it was encouraging to be asked. Her books were well known in Catholic seminaries. *Rediscovering the Bible* had been translated into Spanish in 1944 and — in a shortened version — into Portuguese in 1955. A Spanish edition of *Le dessein de Dieu* appeared in 1952. These books had also become teaching manuals in the Latin American SCMs. On their travels the regional SCM secretaries Mauricio Lopez and Valdo Galland always carried copies, and promoted them widely.

Both for Suzanne and the participants *the* event was the Campos de Jordan meeting. The following year the WCC executive committee met in Buenos Aires, and it brought several ecumenical leaders to the continent. Among them was Madeleine Barot who wrote to Suzanne: "Everybody here and elsewhere is asking for news of you, and speaks with nostalgia about your meetings... Evidently for the student groups in Brazil there is an era before and an era after Suzanne. No need to tell you that Wim, Philip Potter and I in particular have used and abused our links with you." For the two Bible courses in Brazil Suzanne was asked to lead sessions with special emphasis on church-world relationships. To serve as background material the study guide which she had written for the Episcopalians, *The Word and His People* (Greenwich, 1958) was translated into Spanish. The leadership team of the Campos de Jordan meeting challenged the legalistic morality which conservative North American missionaries had impressed on Latin American Protestantism. Suzanne wrote about an incident which became part of the oral tradition of young Latin American Protestants and was shared with the WCC visitors in 1960: "Dance is taboo and these people have dance in their body... When once two or three began some steps of tango, quite innocently I joined with my sticks. Shouts of joy: 'Suzanne has redeemed the tango!'" [4]

It was not just legalistic morality that had to be put in question but also dogmatic positions about the Bible and Christian faith, so that students would be freed to do their own biblical-theological thinking in and for the Latin American situation. In an analysis entitled "Theological Developments in the Brazilian SCM" Richard Shaull, former WSCF chairman who was much involved in Latin American student work, spoke of the impact of the type of Bible study advocated in Suzanne's books: "Students were encouraged to approach the Bible, not as the source of abstract, sterile doctrines, but as the story of God's presence and action in human life and in concrete historical events in the world across the centuries. This led them to reflect on their own historical situation in the light of this special history of God's action in the world, and as they did so, they discovered that they were being addressed. The text of the Bible was no longer a dead letter, a collection of correct ideas and abstract doctrines..."

The students "found themselves responding to a Word they could not ignore, a Word that opened doors to new life for them and led to transformation".[5] About Suzanne's studies at the Campos de Jordan meeting Shaull said that "they focused on such themes as the nature of the biblical story and the presence of God in history" as well as on the biblical message of social justice.

Such studies led to action, and Shaull pointed to the fact that soon the students who were involved in the Latin American revolutionary situation became dissatisfied with the common European type of Bible study, especially when led by academic biblical scholars who did not share Suzanne's openness and curiosity for the realities of the Brazilian situation. European historical critical studies seemed "too technical and cold... The end result was that, precisely when these students most needed the orientation and support our biblical theology had promised, they felt let down by it." In the 1970s a post-Suzanne era began in Latin America in the area of Bible study. Members of Christian base communities interpreted the Bible essentially from the perspective of the poor and in the context of a revolutionary struggle. Suzanne was interested in and challenged by this development. In Paris she maintained contact with Latin American students, but unfortunately could not make a third visit to the continent. It would have been fascinating to see her listening to the liberation theologians and members of the Christian base communities, learning from them and challenging them.

A taste of Africa
On her way to Latin America in early 1959, for the first time in her life Suzanne spent three days on African soil. As a member of the CIMADE management team she visited the foyer and dispensary in Dakar, started by CIMADE in 1955. Difficulties had arisen between the traditional Protestant parish and the CIMADE team members. The free,

dialogical style of collaboration between Africans and Europeans, and between Protestants, Catholics and Muslims in CIMADE work, clashed with the more traditional style of many members of the Protestant congregation. Suzanne had to preside over a frank and difficult discussion between the parish council and the CIMADE team, which led to a provisional separation of work between the two. During her brief stay Suzanne was struck by the dignity of the Senegalese. She had a conversation with Muslim women which introduced her to the problems that come up when the old and the new meet in African society. Through correspondence and two further visits to Dakar Suzanne became a trusted friend of the Dakar CIMADE team.

The Algerian struggle for independence and the French-Algerian war of 1954-62 were constantly on Suzanne's mind. Through newspapers and personal correspondence, for instance with Metzel who visited prisons in Algeria, Suzanne followed this "nightmare" as she often called that war. She was keen to go to Algiers. CIMADE had developed work in various places there, and in May-June 1962 she was sent to visit the CIMADE teams in their difficult situation. She came back with a heavy heart and wrote to Visser 't Hooft: "I fear the Nazi virus is spreading in France. But I am proud of our CIMADE team members... With all our energy we must work to prepare the confessing church of tomorrow."

In 1955 the Swiss publishing house Delachaux-Niestle had asked Suzanne to help with literature for Africa. She also had invitations to lead Bible study courses in the Congo and Kenya, but she was busy and doubted whether she could still make such trips. Through her friendship with the medical missionary Annette Casalis in Northern Rhodesia (now Zambia) and with Inga-Brita Castren, the WSCF travelling secretary for Africa, Suzanne was able to keep herself informed of developments in Africa.

But her real immersion in Africa south of the Sahara came only when she was 74 years old. Hank Crane, the new WSCF secretary for Africa, planned a leadership training course at Mindolo near Kitwe in Zambia, and he asked Suzanne to go over and help. She accepted the challenge. Some seventy students and teachers from Malawi, Rhodesia, Zaire and Zambia participated in the two-week course over New Year 1965-66. Suzanne was not happy with her lectures on biblical theology and the discussions that followed. She felt that what she said did not get through or was misunderstood. This was partly due to the largely fundamentalist background of most participants, and partly because she had not taken sufficiently into account the cultural setting of Africa. Only when she asked the participants to mime a psalm or to play a parable, transposing them into their present setting, did they come alive and their singular gifts find expression. "They are born actors," she wrote, and added: "It can happen that the message of the text is drowned in the comedy of the scene."

She shared with Crane her thoughts about a new way and a fresh content for teaching in Africa: "Two problems have been trotting through my mind ever since: the need for a more adequate language adapted to their form of thought, using as far as possible their categories; and, still more, the fact that we have not convinced them that Jesus Christ has *really* overcome the demonic forces of this world. The students are still in the grip of these forces and it splits their personality dangerously... Hasn't the church put them under the law instead of demonstrating by her life and faith the reality of Christ's victory?"[6]

After the Mindolo course, Suzanne visited friends in the region and was much impressed by the medical ministry of Casalis. She also visited the Victoria Falls near Livingstone. People in Zaire had heard that she was in the region, and a small four-seater plane was sent to fly her from Kitwe over the Katanga to Luluaburg (Kananga) in Zaire where the plane landed on the football field of the United Theological School. There Suzanne was to teach for a week. She had got hold of R.P. Temple's *La philosophie bantoue*, and it made an impact on her teaching: "When I spoke about Jesus, the image of God, there were difficulties in understanding what exactly was meant (one tends to think of a physical resemblance). When I said to them that Jesus is full of the vital force of God and that he communicates this force to us, there is understanding. The day they believe that this force of Jesus is more powerful than all demons and that He has conquered them, they will cease to fear spirits and no longer appeal to witch doctors... As long as they do not have this belief it is dangerous to ask them to break customs which are so deeply rooted in their being."[7]

Suzanne was asked many questions which she could not always answer, and the days in Luluaburg were for her a great learning experience. "I can understand better now why St Paul wrote to the Colossians with such insistence that Christ has nailed to the cross all authorities and powers. It serves little to deny their reality; you must know that they are overcome." The "taste" of Africa stayed with her. She concluded her report to friends: "Are you surprised that Africa has captured my heart? How annoying it is to be 75 years old!" But for many years she continued to conduct Bible studies for African students in her apartment in Paris.

New tasks in Europe

Despite her fascination with people and views in other continents and despite her impatience with French self-sufficiency, Suzanne remained a French woman and a European. Whenever she could get a copy of *Le monde* during her travels she would read it avidly. French and European politics continued to interest her, especially because they had their impact in other places as well — in the Middle East, Indochina, Algeria and the whole of Africa. Suzanne continued to travel and teach in several European regions. In 1962, at the invitation of Kathleen Bliss, she went to England to train Anglican clergy in conducting participatory Bible studies. In 1957 she was in Finland, and that was a new experience for her. Finnish church life was marked by a kind of pietism constantly recharged through various revival movements. She had heard much about the Finnish Lutheran pietist Baron Nicolay and his pioneering Bible study work among students in Russia. During the war she had admired the courage of the Finnish people in their struggle for freedom. The Orthodox Church in Finland, different from that of the Russian emigrants in France, could become a new partner in the search for unity. The Finnish SCM was a full member of the WSCF and at the same time an affiliated member of the conservative-evangelical International Fellowship of Evangelical Students. The growing split between "conservative-evangelical" and "ecumenical" Christians in France and all over the world worried Suzanne increasingly and she saw in Finland a new challenge for the work of unity.

A shy Finnish participant in the first graduate school at Bossey in 1952-53 had won Suzanne's heart: Inga-Brita Castren, later WSCF secretary for Africa. She invited Suzanne to teach several courses at the Järvenpää centre near Helsinki. In her ecumenical memoirs Castren recalls the impact Suzanne's studies made. To see the whole of the biblical message running through the Old and New Testament books, to relate this message to present-day life and history, and especially to hold together a genuine biblical piety and full biblical freedom — all this was new for many Finnish Christians. If Suzanne "redeemed" the tango in Brazil she "redeemed" for some Christian circles in Finland the enjoyment of a game of cards or a glass of wine! Suzanne's book *Le dessein de Dieu* was immediately translated into Finnish and became a teaching manual at Järvenpää.

Another participant at the first graduate school in Bossey, the American Congregational pastor Ken Baker, played an important role in Suzanne's life and work in France during her retirement. He became the director of the foyer and conference centre in Chambon-sur-Lignon, the Protestant village which during the second world war became widely known for its resistance to Nazism and its courage in helping Jews. From 1958, at Baker's invitation, Suzanne led summer vacation Bible courses for adults at the "Accueil". Later Ken, his wife Marion and their children often provided a welcoming and caring home for Suzanne in her old age. In Paris Suzanne rejoined the church of Passy. For Bible study and the liturgical life in the church she worked together with an old friend, Sylvaine Moussat, who had been an assistant to Marc Boegner and Pierre Maury. Occasionally she also taught New Testament at the training school for candidates in mission and conducted courses at the Centre de formation chrétienne (centre for Christian training). She continued to help with French Christian youth movements and to lead sessions at the women's community of Pomeyrol. With the men's community in Taizé her links were somewhat strained, but not for theological reasons. When she left Bossey Suzanne had entrusted her companion Chouky to a friend who lived in Taizé. There Chouky was accused of harrying a lamb and was shot, something Suzanne never quite forgave the brothers.

Suzanne's main teaching and counselling work in France was now done for CIMADE whose management team she had joined in 1958. The work was demanding and exhausting. In a 1958 circular letter she wrote about one of the many CIMADE camps she attended: "Madeleine Barot's unlimited capacity for work which more or less kills everybody except her means that I never stopped from 8 in the morning until midnight: leading Bible study all morning, discussing work with the various teams from lunch to tea time, in session from tea to dinner time and from 8.30 to 11. I retire about midnight, leaving the others to further talks or outings. I felt that whoever survived CIMADE could survive anything."

In the 1950s and 1960s Suzanne was at times unhappy that in Europe the enthusiasm for Bible study had declined both in youth movements and local parishes. It was therefore a great joy for her when in France the work of the Equipes de recherche biblique (groups for biblical studies) began. This movement was initiated by a brilliant young woman, Françoise Florentin, and such scholars as Wilhelm Vischer and Pierre Bonnard were involved. Suzanne was a member of the committee from its beginning in 1961. The aim of the movement was to help Protestant lay people, and later Roman Catholics and agnostics as well, to do their own biblical research, and thus to relate academic biblical scholarship in theological faculties to the everyday life of Christians. From 1965 onwards the teams became part of the French Protestant Federation.[8]

Suzanne not only contributed to the work, she also learned much from it. Collaboration with a new generation of pastors and lay people who were leading Bible studies and also with a new generation of biblical scholars had an impact on her own biblical teaching and writing. When in 1963 Florentin came back from her research work in Jerusalem and began to teach Hebrew to French peasants so that they could study the Old Testament in the original language, Suzanne was greatly impressed and wrote to Visser 't Hooft: "Before this passionate Hebrew specialist I feel like a very ignorant old woman." However, far from being discouraged, she found this a stimulus for her own biblical teaching.

Serving the ecumenical movement

During retirement much of Suzanne's work was still related to the ecumenical world organizations. Soon after leaving Bossey she became a member of the board of the Ecumenical Institute, then chaired by Kathleen Bliss, where she worked together with such old friends as Paul Evdokimov and Francis Ayres, the leading member of the Parishfield community, and with new friends, especially Aarne Siirala, the director of the Finnish lay training centre at Järvenpää. Besides the annual board meetings Bossey often invited her to teach at conferences and courses. She was also on the board of *The Ecumenical Review*, contributed several articles and book reviews, and was a critical reader of what was published. Once she wrote to Visser 't Hooft: "Wim, your article raises a problem for me: not once do you mention the Holy Spirit. Yet the third person of the Trinity has a very special role to play in the ecumenical movement and our Christology should not ignore this."[9]

Suzanne was always ready to respond to requests from the WCC Youth department, especially in the training of work camp leaders. She followed with keen interest the work of the Laity department, and the secretariat for biblical studies which was created in 1971. After her exposure to Africa she took a special interest in how this WCC secretariat responded to various approaches to Bible study in different cultures. With her strong views on the role of women, marriage and men-women relationships one would have expected Suzanne to work closely with the WCC Department of Cooperation between Men and Women in Church and Society, especially because Kathleen Bliss and Madeleine Barot played outstanding roles there. This, however, did not happen — women's issues were not a major concern for her.

During these years Suzanne had only limited contacts with the World YWCA. The ecumenical organization with which she maintained close contact and which called most often on her services was the WSCF. In July 1960 she had been a speaker at the large WSCF teaching conference in Strasbourg which had gathered old and new leaders from all continents. Like many others she felt the change of climate which heralded the student revolts of 1968. Especially European, North and Latin American SCMs assumed in the late sixties radical theological, ideological and political positions which frightened and even alienated many "senior friends" of the Federation. Suzanne did not agree with many of these positions, but more than other former WSCF leaders she kept in touch and tried to understand. In an article written for the 75th anniversary of the WSCF in 1970 she welcomed the decentralization of Federation work in six regions and expressed her interest in the new ways of leadership training and the search for new styles of life. With deep sympathy she tried to understand what the new leaders of the Federation taught about "Christian presence", "humanization" and "revolution". Where other "old hands" tended to be critical and judgmental, Suzanne listened, questioned and wished well. Concluding her article she wrote: "Beyond all doubt the young Federation of 1970 is listening to its own time. Let us hope that it will also listen with the same passion to the Lord of history, and that the Lord may use it for developing in these new times that new theology, that new university, that new national and international justice for which all of us are longing." [10]

NOTES

[1] Henri Leenhardt, letter of 6 July 1950 to SdD, and typed transcript of Dean Leenhardt's speech of September 1950.

[2] SdD, letter of 30 August 1954 to B.R. Lacy.

[3] Chambron, interview with SdD, transcript, pp.33f.

[4] SdD, circular letter of 7 April 1959, p.5.

[5] Richard Shaull, multicopied draft paper on *Theological Developments in the Brazilian SCM*, written for a consultation on "Bible and Theology in the History of the WSCF", Bossey, April 1993.

[6] SdD, letter of 11 March 1966 to Hank Crane.

[7] SdD, typed circular for friends on *Cinq semaines en Afrique: quelques réflexions*, 1966.

[8] Cf. the chapter on "Les équipes de recherche biblique en France", written by Simone Frutiger, in SdD, *Le renouveau biblique: hier et aujourd'hui*, II, Neuchâtel, 1969, pp.64-68.

[9] SdD, letter of 5 December 1955 to Visser 't Hooft.

[10] SdD, "Trois quarts de siècle dans le monde étudiant", *L'illustré protestant*, no. 188, September 1970, p.15.

12
Biblical Witness

Suzanne was once compared to the sculpture of Pythagoras under the nativity scenes in the royal portal of the cathedral in Chartres. Like a child tracing his first lines he sits there bent over his tablet, all attention and humility. "So I often thought of Suzanne: shrunk in her chair, before her typewriter or among a Bible study group. With humble but persistent and obstinate attention, like that of the Pythagoras of Chartres, she works at deciphering the biblical witness not *for* others but *with* others." [1] Simone Frutiger, who made this comparison at a thanksgiving service, had known Suzanne for almost forty years and had worked with her closely in her biblical teaching ministry. The following comments on Suzanne as a biblical witness owe much to her.

Scholars and animators

Two exegetes, Jules Breitenstein and Lucien Gauthier, had started the young Suzanne off on her journey of biblical exploration. Among her four main mentors in the late 1920s and 1930s — Henry B. Sharman, Karl Barth, Pierre de Bérulle and Paul Evdokimov — none was, strictly speaking, a biblical scholar. This is significant. Suzanne would never allow either the Bible or herself to be imprisoned in the ivory tower of academia. During and after the second world war she again worked closely with Old and New Testament scholars, especially Wilhelm Vischer and Pierre Bonnard, but she did so with the sole aim of better equipping herself to help ordinary Christians, and all seekers, to discover for themselves God's word for their particular world, profession and life situation. Suzanne's vocation was clearly that of the Bible study animator and not that of the biblical researcher. She knew that an animator risks becoming a manipulator when neglecting the biblical texts, and the messages such texts address to readers are lost sight of. Therefore she always remained a student, keenly interested in what was happening in biblical scholarship.

While teaching at the Ecumenical Institute in Bossey Suzanne participated in the first fully ecumenical study process on the authority and interpretation of the Bible. Even before its official inauguration the World Council of Churches had gathered groups of outstanding biblical and systematic theologians, Protestant and Orthodox, mostly from Europe and North America. Among them were C.H. Dodd, Karl Barth and Reinhold Niebuhr. They were asked to help the WCC by reflecting on "the authority of the Bible for the churches' social and political message today".[2] In 1947 an interim report appeared, along with the papers and conclusions from the first two consultations, one held in London in 1946 and the other at Bossey in 1947. Suzanne participated in the second one, the only woman and the only one without formal theological training. The consultation summed up its findings in seven theses which clearly reflected the type of biblical teaching developed in the WSCF message study before the war and which was tested in the struggle of the Confessing Church in Germany. The authority of the Bible was seen as derived from the authority of Christ, who is confessed as the centre of the whole Bible and the one through whom God reconciles and rules the world. It was probably Suzanne who proposed, and convinced the group of scholars about the need, to include the thesis that it is the special duty of the church "to bring its members to a clear awareness of the meaning of the lordship of Christ for every aspect of their life, including their daily work".[3]

Suzanne never claimed any expertise as a biblical exegete. She had only limited access to the original biblical languages, and no special training in either biblical archeology or ancient Near Eastern history. Wisely she refrained from joining the scholarly debates on controversial exegetical questions. Her unique contribution to biblical scholarship lay in seeing and presenting the multi-splendoured biblical testimonies as one whole. She listened, in the first place, sympathetically, critically and meditatively, to the biblical witnesses themselves, and then also to the scholarly debate about these witnesses. Then she responded with her own gifts to what she had recognized, as early as 1920, as a fundamental need: the preparation of Bible study material and the writing of biblical commentaries for lay people. Besides the thousands of much-used Bible study outlines, she also wrote commentaries: on Paul's letter to the Philippians entitled *Towards Fullness of Life*, on Matthew's Gospel entitled *Saint Matthew*, and on the letters of John entitled *This We Know*.[4]

Biblical scholars could learn certain fundamental lessons from Suzanne's writings. She used to say that real exegetes never take themselves seriously, because they know their limitations and are aware of the fact that their work is based on the work of many others. She would not allow herself or others to manipulate a biblical text by prematurely projecting into it dogmatic, ecclesiastical or personal interpretations. Such honesty would not allow Suzanne to take up earlier Bible study outlines or commentaries and simply brush them up for use in a new situation. Whenever possible she listened again to the biblical witnesses and to fresh scholarly debates about them, while taking into account also the questions of the new time and environment within which the study on these old texts was to take place. She never avoided or left aside questions from the world or the debate about the word, or new questions or challenges from the biblical witnesses themselves. The different language editions of her biblical commentaries were not simple translations but re-edited new versions which she often submitted to academic exegetes for criticism before finalizing them for publication.

The most remarkable example of such rewriting are the two volumes of *Le renouveau biblique, hier et aujourd'hui* (Neuchatel, 1969). More than twenty years after the first publication of the French version in 1945, Suzanne, now almost 76 years old, was asked by her editor to check the book with a view to bringing out a new edition. She sought the advice of a few scholars well informed on new developments in both biblical scholarship and the methodology of Bible study. Françoise Smyth-Florentin of the Equipes de recherche biblique felt that a total rewrite was needed. The Benedictine exegete Jacques Dupont, who had also reread the 1945 edition of *Renouveau biblique*, disagreed. This would require an almost superhuman effort, he said. Moreover, "we must take account of the role this work has played in the history of the biblical movement; it represents an important step and has its value as such. It is a 'historical' document and should not be tampered with."[5] Father Dupont made concrete suggestions on how to rework parts of the manuscript, without attempting a total revision. Nevertheless, Suzanne decided to rewrite the whole book and, with the tenacity of the little Pythagoras, she started work on what became a two-volume manual. Frutiger, who was associated with this rewriting, recalls how in the process she learned unique lessons in intellectual honesty, persistency, humility and humour from the author who remained a student of the Bible till the end of her life.

In the first volume Suzanne dealt with the question: "What is the Bible?" She summed up what had been learned about the Bible, as both human words and God's word, in biblical scholarship and in the ecumenical movement. She emphasized the unity of the two Testaments and the ways in which the Bible shapes Christian ethics. The earlier survey on how the Bible had functioned and was interpreted in the early church and down the centuries, in the various Christian confessions and in the ecumenical movement, was expanded and a new chapter on Bible translation and distribution was added. The second volume addressed the issue of how to read the Bible. Suzanne there summed up her own experience of various study approaches, and included concrete examples of the work of younger Catholic and Protestant biblical animators. The clearly-written final product of some 400 pages concluded with an up-to-date bibliography.

The book dealt with many of the old themes, but it was now a new book. The editor wanted to give it a new title, but Suzanne was against it; she did not want to hide the fact that it was the old book, extensively revised. Perhaps that explains why it was not widely used and — except for an Italian edition — not translated into other languages. People thought that it was simply a paperback version of a slightly revised edition of the 1945 classic. Suzanne herself had a certain unease about the new book. The exegetical work accomplished by biblical scholars after the second world war had been so extensive and diverse that she could only give "a summary of summaries". Nevertheless, the *Renouveau biblique: hier et aujourd'hui* still remains the best informed, most readable and concise resource on this vast subject, although today it would have to be rewritten once again to include developments since the 1960s.

Besides their intellectual honesty, Suzanne's teaching and writing are also marked by their total lack of polemic. Not that fundamental disagreements in scholarly hypotheses or differences arising out of confessional and cultural diversities are toned down or glossed over. With her "Gallic" preference for synthesis she takes into account diverse opinions and tries to reconcile them through a common search for a fuller truth. The only polemic she accepted and practised was that of the biblical witnesses who continue to challenge, judge and convert our human thinking and action.

As a biblical animator Suzanne drew thousands of lay people, pastors and priests around the world into a corporate study of the biblical witnesses. Even in parts of the world she never visited, China, Australia and New Zealand, for example, her teaching had its impact through her books, and even more through people who had been trained by her. An example of this is Suzanne's indirect influence on the extraordinary development of Bible study in China since the 1980s in which two of her "students", the Chinese church leader K.H. Ting (a former WSCF secretary) and his wife Siu May Kuo, play such an outstanding role.[6] Suzanne also challenged biblical scholars to become animators, calling them to come out of their academic isolation and in-group concerns. In Bible seminars during and after the war and while teaching at Bossey she asked biblical scholars to help her with training sessions. Her clear and concise style made her writing accessible to all intelligent readers whatever their training, unlike the often indigestible language of scholars. Suzanne's questions and analytical comments forced exegetes to think through difficult exegetical problems until they could express their findings, both convictions reached and remaining uncertainties, in a generally understandable way.

Biblical ways of Bible study

Biblical scholars are so fascinated by the content and diversity of the biblical testimonies they explore that they tend to ignore the methods by which these testimonies are communicated to them and by which they themselves can effectively communicate the result of their research. In practice this means that they usually use the same old methods of analysis, lectures and academic papers. At the other extreme, biblical animators are so fascinated by the variety of mediums with which one can communicate a given message that much or all of the message is often lost in the process. Suzanne met something of this latter type when in North America she came into contact with the group dynamics movement, which is based on psychological studies about how human groups function and on the factors that both facilitate communication and militate against it. She was reluctant to apply the insights gained in group dynamics to the practice of Bible study. In a letter from the US in 1955 she complained about the "group dynamics" orientation and the danger of the method replacing the content. She knew that method and message, medium and content, could not be easily separated. However, before her exposure to Africa Suzanne was probably not sufficiently aware of how much her own ways of animating Bible study communicated not only what she saw as the substance of true biblical testimonies but also much of her own European background and culture.

For her the Bible remained essentially a literary document in the form of printed texts. She knew of course that long before printing was invented the Bible had existed as a series of manuscripts, often illuminated manuscripts where the image complements and interprets the written text. She was also aware that for most of these manuscripts there was a prehistory of oral tradition when the biblical testimonies had been told, recited, sung and communicated through gestures, liturgical acts and symbols. Nevertheless, in her ministry of biblical teaching Suzanne worked almost exclusively with texts, with the literary medium of biblical communication.

In group Bible study she generally started with the reading of the text, then asked questions which helped participants to examine carefully what really had been said. She would add some comments on the time, the circumstances and the first hearers/readers of the passage. This led to common work by all group members to discern the main affirmations of the text. Finally they would discuss together how this particular text "spoke" to them in their own time and life situation. In her very first report about Bible study in 1920 Suzanne had described this approach, and with minor variations she followed it throughout her life. She conducted such studies of the text by the Socratic method, proceeding through questions that stimulated a common search. She had seen this way of teaching practised by Henry B. Sharman, but long before that she had observed it in the teaching of Jesus himself. Her method of teaching, though strongly marked by her Protestant and European background, was a biblical way of doing Bible study.

Suzanne's active participation in sessions of the Equipes de recherche biblique confirmed her in working mainly with texts — with the Bible as a literary document. There she became much more aware of the diversity of the biblical testimonies, the fact, for instance, that each evangelist contributed his own particular testimony about the life, ministry, death and resurrection of Jesus. Like Bonnard she began to speak about the "Matthean Jesus" in distinction to the Jesus of Mark or Luke or John. She also learned about ways of study which complemented the more historical approach she had used so far. Applying methods of literary analysis to the study of biblical texts, one can discern basic story-structures, for instance in the healing stories of the gospels. The original author and the historical context in which and for which the text was originally written then become less important. The text immediately addresses the contemporary reader. As one becomes sensitive to these basic structures, and especially to the elements in a given text which do not conform to the usual pattern of story-telling, biblical texts are suddenly seen in a new light. Suzanne remained very hesitant to use such methods of literary analysis.

What fascinated her was a rediscovered diversity of literary genres in the Bible: narrative texts with parables and cycles of stories; juridical texts with prescriptions and prohibitions, formulas, for instance, of curse and blessing; liturgical texts with hymns, prayers and gestures of worship; wisdom texts with proverbs, stories of spiritual edification and riddles; prophetic and apocalyptic texts with their oracles, visions and symbolic acts. Suzanne also knew and respected the diverse ways of interpretation found in the Bible itself. So she protested when in the ecumenical study process on the authority and interpretation of the Bible a drafter wanted to censor all typological interpretation, whereby events in the Old Testament are seen to foreshadow as types key events in Jesus' life: "The way in which you dismiss typology in one sentence seems to me unfair. I don't think that a typological interpretation implies necessarily a 'static' conception of history at all. That typology has its place in Old and New Testament thinking... A serious historian must take seriously the Bible *as interpreted by the Bible itself.* That this was not done is the fundamental criticism made by many present-day scholars against the historical school. They blame this school for having started from its own conception of historical accuracy instead of trying to understand what truth the biblical writer meant to convey. Of this, the disregard for any typological interpretation is only one example among many." [7]

The different literary genres reflect different ways of biblical communication and pedagogy. These genres must therefore be not only distinguished and analyzed, they can also be practised in doing Bible study. This leads animators and participants to use other than literary ways of exploration. While the testimonies of biblical witnesses must always be checked in the literary medium in which they are now transmitted to us, these testimonies need to be freed from print. They must again become the audible word spoken and heard, the visible word seen and meditated, the enacted word in liturgical worship, in prophetic acts and in the decisions of daily life.

For a long time Suzanne remained hesitant to use non-literary ways of Bible study. This gradually changed when she had to lead studies for groups in cultures different from that of the European, mainly French, student circles with which for the most part she had worked so far. In the southern states of the USA, in Brazil, and especially in Africa she was challenged to reconsider her ways of teaching.

As I was at that time facing a similar challenge and had long conversations and exchanges of letters with Suzanne about methods of Bible study, an autobiographical paragraph may not be out of place here. In SCM work and a youth leaders' course at Bossey in 1948 I was introduced to Suzanne's ways of Bible study. Later, I used them in

Indonesia as a theological teacher in central Celebes and as a student worker in East Java. In 1953 the Indonesian church asked me to go to the isolated mountain and island area of Luwuk-Banggai on the east coast of Celebes to organize biblical teaching among some 30,000 Christians who had been baptized without receiving adequate baptismal instruction. About two-thirds of them were exclusively oral communicators (whom we pejoratively call non-readers, illiterates). While still following the basic pattern of teaching I learned from Suzanne, it now became necessary to use other, less literary ways of Bible study such as story-telling, drama, mime, drawing, gestures, songs and symbols. Out of this meeting with oral communicators grew a catechism for "illiterates" (1955), a publication on *The Communication of the Gospel to Illiterates* (1957) and, influenced partly by this experience, from 1971 the biblical studies secretariat in the WCC where I could further explore and practise various ways of doing Bible study in different countries and cultural settings.[8]

A report about my work in Indonesia was part of the input at the joint WSCF/Bossey consultation on "Ecumenism and the Bible" in 1955, which Suzanne had helped to prepare.[9] As soon as she heard about the catechism for "illiterates" she wanted a translation of the Indonesian text which accompanies the drawings of the catechism. She began work on a French translation and adaptation of the booklet, and she wanted me to help in developing a simplified and more visual version of her *Dessein de Dieu* for Africa. Because it took a long time for her to recover from her accident in the USA in 1955, and because both of us had more urgent work, we were not able to take up that joint writing project. Nevertheless, Suzanne now began to explore non-literary ways of Bible study also — role-play, drawing and mime — in her teaching in the USA, Latin America and Africa. When rewriting *Renouveau biblique* she described in the second volume experiments where various literary genres were not only analyzed but actually applied as methods and media for biblical teaching.

All the same Suzanne maintained a healthy critical attitude towards such less intellectual and less literary approaches. In 1969 she wrote to me: "I am interested in your efforts to combine art/image with a biblical theme. This is a field I have never ventured into. Sometimes it makes me sad that so many 'tricks' must be used in order to interest people in the word of God." Rightly or wrongly, I could never fully convince Suzanne that non-literary ways of doing Bible study might be more than "tricks".

Towards a biblical theology

Responding to the invitation to become the first visiting professor at Union Theological Seminary in Richmond, Virginia, Suzanne was quite clear about her limitations in the field of theological training. Her vocation, she said, was "to make the Bible live for laymen and to help them to see it as a whole and to interpret the parts in the light of the whole". This was indeed her great contribution in the field both of biblical animation and biblical scholarship. The worldwide response to her book *Le dessein de Dieu* showed that it met a real need, in a way which the specialized scholars had not done. The individual trees hid the forest. The dispersed mosaic of isolated texts, chosen either because of personal preferences or dogmatic presuppositions, obscured the testimony of biblical witnesses. "What is often missing today for lay people's intelligent understanding of the Bible are views [note the plural] of the whole which allow them to detect the main lines of a passage, a book, a given author. If it is true that the texts must be studied to be well understood, it is also true that with regard to the biblical witness the part cannot be fully understood except in the light of the whole. It is the task of biblical theology to help the thinking of an author to emerge, and to place it within the whole of revelation. For a Christian it is in the revelation of God in Jesus Christ that all the testimonies of the writers of the Old and the New Testament receive their ultimate meaning. Therefore lay people need both an initiation to the study of a *text* and a solid *biblical theology*."[10] Needless to say, it is not only lay people who need such a solid biblical theology: pastors, priests and theological teachers must also see the whole, and they often fail to do so.

The way Suzanne brought all the various testimonies of the Bible together in her *Dessein de Dieu* was by taking salvation history, as expounded by Oscar Cullmann, as the main thread. In answer to the observation that there are many biblical theologies, not just one, she said in 1971: "Yes, this is true, but I think that at that moment the book responded to a need. But I still believe that there is a line (in this I am very Cullmannian), a thread of salvation which goes right through the Bible. This is a major thread; of course, there are others." Even before writing her main book on biblical theology, Suzanne did not make individual studies of isolated texts but always placed them in a wider context. In 1938 she published an essay in which the love of God became the theme which held the various biblical testimonies together.[11] In *The Witnessing Community*, (Philadelphia, 1958), which brought together her lectures at Union Theological Seminary in Richmond, the testimony of the people of Israel and the church in the world became the focus for seeing the Bible as a whole. Earlier she had chosen the affirmation of freedom to draw together the various biblical testimonies, in her study on *Free Men*. [12]

Suzanne's last attempt to bring together what she heard the many different biblical witnesses testify was her series of lectures at the American Baptist Bible conference at Green Lake in 1966, *God's Word in Today's World*. [13] She took up two basic biblical questions, namely the world's challenge: "Where is thy God?", and God's challenge: "Man, where are you?", and commented on three fundamental human and biblical quests, those for justice, freedom and truth. This led to a final affirmation which for Suzanne always remained the centre of the whole Bible: "Christ, our hope".

"No longer can we speak of *the* theology of the Old or the New Testament: there are many," Suzanne wrote towards the end of the 1960s. For other representatives of the biblical renewal movement of the 1930s this diversity discovered in biblical scholarship seemed to be a threat. Suzanne accepted it with joy. It responded to her love of freedom, and she immediately drew out its consequences: "This freedom of biblical interpretation means that the same freedom should prevail today in any union of churches and the ecumenical movement."

In the decades following the publication of *Dessein de Dieu* biblical exegesis became increasingly more fragmentary and specialized. Affirmations about *the* biblical message were quite rightly rejected as not taking sufficient account of the great diversity among and tensions between the various biblical faith traditions. [14] No scholar dared to work on a biblical theology which would cover both the Old and the New Testament. The pendulum is now beginning to swing back. In scholarly journals we are seeing articles which point to the need for a renewed biblical theology. Brevard S. Childs and others strongly emphasize that biblical passages and books must be read and interpreted within the framework of the biblical canon. [15] Suzanne rejoiced when in the 1960s she read Gerhard von Rad's Old Testament theology which ends with a long chapter where the lines of Old Testament faith traditions are drawn out into the New Testament. But did she fully realize how diverse the biblical testimonies are? Her own various "views of the whole" are all variations on the salvation history perspective. What would she have said to von Rad's study on the wisdom literature where he showed that for the people of Israel wisdom represented an alternative theological option, standing apart and in tension with the more familiar historical and prophetic traditions? How would she have evaluated a biblical theology like that of Samuel Terrien, where God's presence and wisdom more than salvation become the focal point for seeing the whole? These and other new attempts at outlining a biblical theology based on present exegetical insights appeared shortly before or after Suzanne's death and she was unable to read them. But she would certainly have liked Claus Westermann's study where he juxtaposes "the saving God and history" with "the blessing God and creation". [16]

In her last essay, published in 1971, Suzanne made a contribution to the new quest for seeing the Bible as a whole. Just as she had done in her first published lecture of 1912, she began with a question: "Is a systematic theology still possible?" [17] Her initial answer was that in a world shaped by scientists and technicians, a systematic theology based on philosophical language would remain the monopoly of a scholarly elite and that such teaching on Christian faith could not reach the church membership as it should. She suggested we might be in a period where God remained silent, an experience which the prophets had long before us. For her the only way to come by a comprehensive view of Christian faith was to elaborate a new biblical theology through exegesis. "I am deeply convinced that, because of its realistic and practical approach, the biblical view on human beings and on history, and even on God, is more accessible to many of our contemporaries than the often abstruse philosophical-theological theories we often offer them." Suzanne was implicitly alluding to the death-of-God theology which she had come across in the USA, and to ideologically conditioned views of Jesus as an existentialist or a Marxist which she encountered among students in France. Despite her great concern to draw out socio-political implications from the prophets and the gospel texts she consistently rejected a unidimensional reduction of the Bible to a political gospel. For the elaboration of a new biblical theology Suzanne showed the way forward in three directions.

Biblical theologians must start not from dogmatic or ideological presuppositions but from sober and serious exegetical work. Exegesis is itself constantly conditioned by conscious or unconscious dogmatic and ideological convictions. Suzanne's Latin American friends had taught her this lesson. Yet a given biblical text, if studied and meditated upon with an open mind, constantly keeps in check such dogmatic and ideological biases.

Biblical theologians should take seriously the many faith traditions in the Bible. These different theological currents developed, in the course of biblical history, not in a vacuum but in reponse to specific religious and socio-economic environments. For each biblical faith tradition its sources and its milieu must be studied in order to discover its basic testimony and meaning.

Biblical theologians must recognize the fact that the witnesses of the Bible always spoke and acted in and for a given milieu and time. The faith traditions as we receive them are formulated ad hoc, for a certain language and mental structure. They are not a set of timeless and general truths. These transmitted faith traditions must be translated and focused on witness in present-day language and mental structures so that they can function in constantly-new situations for teaching, confessing, converting and celebrating. "The systematic theologies of the future will have to be elaborated on the basis of these biblical theologies, taken in their basic meaning, their diversity and their unity." Each synthesis will remain provisional and will vary in different cultural milieus and continents.

Suzanne knew the limitations of all human perception and our great need for the help of the Holy Spirit. "Now we see in a mirror, dimly, but then we will see face to face. Now I only know in part; then I will know fully, even as I have been fully known" (1 Cor. 13:12). She therefore ended her essay with a saying dear to the Orthodox: "A theologian is the one who knows how to pray."

"And He is lifted up"

Prayer was at the heart of Suzanne's work in biblical animation and biblical scholarship. She continuously went from study to meditation and prayer and from there to teaching and prophetic action. "To meditate on a scene of the gospel means to 'see' it, to mingle with the crowd which gathers around Jesus, this thirsty crowd which, like us, seeks immediate and practical deliverance. To meditate means to see Jesus looking at the crowd, at the rich young man, at Zaccheus, at the adulterous woman. It means to lay ourselves open to this look in his eyes which questions us and perceives us as we are. It means to follow Jesus on the way that leads to the cross." [18]

In meditation Suzanne returned to her first meeting with Jesus. The stained-glass Christ of the church in Niederbronn had reached her in a non-literary way, and there also had happened that mysterious reversal of roles: the child looking at Christ had suddenly felt that this Christ was looking at her, questioning and comforting her. Suzanne liked to compare this type of meditation with the way medieval artists became participants of what they painted by including a portrait of themselves as a small figure almost hidden in a corner of the painting. By seeing and exposing ourselves to God's presence we are slowly being changed into God's image and we become part of the cloud of biblical witnesses. Like Job and the psalmists we need not conform to conventional piety but can join in their prayers which often are cries out of the depth, daring to question even their Creator's wisdom. But when they become aware of God's presence and experience grace, their lamentation changes into thanksgiving and praise.

Lest such meditation be misunderstood as an escape into passivity Suzanne immediately emphasizes that "the 'contemplatives' of the Bible are active, fully involved in the problems and the battles of their world. Their relationship with God is the viaticum which makes them wrestlers in the service of God in the concrete realities of history."

Long before writing her first meditational book, *L'heure de l'offrande*, Suzanne had pointed to the centrality of prayer. The world day of prayer of the WSCF, the passion weeks and the weeks of prayer for Christian unity were for her high points of spiritual struggle. She had helped many others to enter into this meditative seeing and biblical praying, especially through her work on the two WSCF worship books *Venite Adoremus*, in translating the prayers of Dietrich Bonhoeffer into French, and through the many retreats she led. Now, near the end of her active life, Suzanne wrote her meditations on John's gospel, *L'heure de l'élévation: à l'écoute de Saint Jean*. [19] She had not worked so long on any other book. From her early years there are notes, meditations and prayers on John's gospel in her journals. During her visit to Palestine in 1929 she looked at the places she visited through the eyes of the Jesus of the fourth gospel, and at the end of that stay she wrote in her journal: "Have memorized John 15. My God, how much have I in all respects been privileged during the whole of this journey. How You surround and protect me!" In Passion week 1931 she memorized daily texts from John 6-12. A year later it was again John's gospel on which she meditated. Jesus' waiting for his hour of suffering and glorification seems to have been constantly present in her mind.

When finally she sent the manuscript of *L'heure de l'élévation* to the printer, she wondered whether she had done the right thing. She felt that life in the 1960s was far too hectic for such a book. It seemed to her that people were not ready to listen, to read, to note down what they read and understood, and even less ready to memorize and interiorize. Yet only in this way could the meditated word become a ferment that would change

their lives. Suzanne's meditations on John's gospel did not receive the same enthusiastic response as her earlier volume of meditations on the synoptic gospels. It was an Anglican member of an ashram, a religious community in India, who wrote to her: "I have read all your books, Suzanne, but this one beats them all. It's not really written to be read, is it, but more to be prayed; you open a chink in a window and we catch a glimpse of something we have never seen before."
This second volume of meditations is written in such concise and poetic prose that it is difficult to summarize. The following is a brief passage from the introduction:

> The apostle John writes like Rembrandt paints: all is contrast of shadow and light.
> Jesus is in the centre, standing in an orb of light.
> All the faces turned towards him are lighted up.
> Those who turn from him are in darkness.

> Believing in the Son is passing from darkness to light, from death to life.
> That is why all is submitted to him.
> Just as he is altogether submitted to his Father.
> He is the divine Word made flesh.
> His work is to establish the new form of worship, in spirit and in truth:
> the new temple — his body;
> the new baptism — baptism of water and of the Spirit;
> the new Passover — his flesh and his blood
> given for the life of the world.
> He is the nourishing Bread, the thirst-quenching Water,
> the life-giving Wine.

> Heavenly liturgy, made incarnate.
> Transfigured matter, infused with life by the Spirit.
> An earnest of eternity.

NOTES

[1] Simone Frutiger, "Suzanne de Diétrich et la Bible", *CIMADE Information*, no. 23, February-March 1981, p.11, and "Suzanne de Diétrich: son rôle dans le renouveau biblique du XXe siècle", recorded lecture on the occasion of the deposit of the Suzanne de Diétrich Papers, Strasbourg, 23 February 1990.

[2] A. Richardson & W. Schweitzer, eds, *Biblical Authority for Today*, London, 1951; and Ellen Flesseman-van Leer, ed., *The Bible: Its Authority and Interpretation in the Ecumenical Movement*, Geneva, WCC, 1980, with a descriptive account of this study process and its reports from 1949, 1963, 1967, 1971 and 1978.

[3] Multicopied document "From the Bible to the Modern World: Two Conference Reports", Geneva, 1947, p.111.

[4] Respectively: French, 1942, English, Philadelphia, 1966; Richmond, UK, 1961, French in 1965; and Richmond, UK, 1963, French in 1964.

[5] Jacques Dupont, letter of 13 December 1966 to F. Smyth-Florentin, and SdD, letter of 22 December 1966 to Dupont.

[6] K.H. Ting, *How To Study the Bible?*, Chinese original, 1980, English Hong Kong, 1981. S.M. Kuo, *Journey through the Bible*, Nanjing, 1990.

[7] SdD, letter of 8 June 1949 to Wolfgang Schweitzer.

[8] H.-R. Weber, *Kamu ini terang dunia* (catechism), Jakarta, 1955; *The Communication of the Gospel to Illiterates*, London, 1957; *Experiments with Bible Study*, Geneva, WCC, 1981.

[9] "Ecumenism and the Bible", *The Student World*, 1956, pp.32-39,78-82.

[10] SdD, *Le renouveau biblique: hier et aujourd'hui*, II, pp.9f.

[11] SdD, "L'amour de Dieu", *Le semeur*, May-June 1938, pp.370-397.

[12] French, 1957; English, Philadelphia/London, 1961.

[13] Valley Forge, PA, 1967.

[14] In the ecumenical study process on the authority and interpretation of the Bible, the diversity of biblical testimonies was particularly emphasized in the 1967 Bristol report on "The Significance of the Hermeneutical Problem for the Ecumenical Movement"; E. Flesseman-van Leer, *op. cit.*, pp.30-41.

[15] B.C. Childs, *Introduction to the Old Testament as Scripture*, London, 1979, and *The New Testament as Canon*, London, 1984.

[16] The books referred to are Gerhard von Rad, *Old Testament Theology*, 2 vols, Edinburgh, 1965, German Munich, 1957-60, and *Wisdom in Israel*, London, 1972, German *Weisheit in Israel*, Neukirchen-Vluyn, 1970 — Samuel Terrien, *The Elusive Presence: Toward a New Biblical Theology*, San Francisco, 1978 — Claus Westermann, *Elements of Old Testament Theology*, Atlanta, 1982, German Göttingen, 1978.

[17] SdD, "Une dogmatique est-elle encore possible?", essay in honour of Jean Bosc, *Foi et vie*, 1971, pp.120-27.

[18] SdD, *Le renouveau biblique*, II, pp.18f.

[19] Neuchâtel, 1966; English *And He Is Lifted Up: Meditations on the Gospel of John*, Philadelphia, 1969.

13
Towards Fullness of Life

"Now that's enough!" With one of her typical impatient reactions
Suzanne suddenly interrupted the celebration her friends from the Equipes
de recherche biblique had organized for her eightieth birthday. They had
spoken about many events in Suzanne's life, and the joy and the insights
with which she had enriched their own lives. "Now that's enough! It's the
future of the church and the world that interests me." Not that she did not
enjoy the celebration. She did. She liked the company of friends, and she
enjoyed a good meal and French wine. And shortly after her birthday she
wrote: "If you have so many friends, it's fun to be 80."

Coping with old age

When she was twenty, Suzanne went to see an old aunt who was
almost totally deaf. Afterwards, writing to a friend, she talked about her
fear of growing old. Despite their congenital defects the de Dietrichs had
a robust constitution. Suzanne was afraid of growing old and helpless, but
she loved life too much to long for an early death. Her radiant personality
made people forget her physical condition. Once, during the second
world war in a group mainly of medical students, discussion centred on
the question of euthanasia. They had heard that in Nazi Germany
mentally and physically handicapped persons were being eliminated. The
students immediately spoke against such practices, but Suzanne, who led
the discussion, felt their arguments were merely emotional and not
supported by reason. She gave a whole series of argument in favour of
euthanasia in order to challenge the group. At the end she said: "Of course
you realize that if euthanasia were practised in our countries I would not
be here. And I would be very sorry." There was complete silence. During
the whole discussion nobody had thought of Suzanne as a handicapped
person. One participant recalled: "We were so taken by the vitality of her
face that we completely forgot the rest."

The "rest", Suzanne's physical problems, became more troublesome
with advancing age. "I am 64 years old: the age when one begins to look

backwards — and forwards also: towards eternity, that great mystery."
For three months Suzanne had been bedridden, in a hospital room in the
USA. There she wrote her "Reflections of an old woman", a ten-page
piece, difficult to decipher and deeply moving. It was only the accident in
July 1955 at Parishfield that made her stop the hectic rhythm of work of
her retirement years. "Blessed be this room," she wrote at the end of her
stay in the hospital. "I have suffered in it, miseries of the body and
emptiness of the soul. But I have known in it hours of peace and extraordinary joy, too. And the friends, the marvellous friends!" Suzanne
often spoke of these months as a period of special grace; she learned there
how to cope with old age.

The friends: she felt surrounded by their prayers and she prayed daily
for them. Part of Suzanne's "Reflections" consists simply of names,
beginning with those who had already preceded her beyond the veil: Alex
de Faye, Charles Grauss, Natacha Evdokimov, Théo Preiss, and so many
others in "that company which comes nearer and becomes ever more alive
as eternity approaches". Also recalled are those who inspired and encouraged her in her spiritual journey, among them Jules Breitenstein, Henri
Bois, Marc Boegner, Pierre Maury, Charles Westphal and Willem Visser
't Hooft ("who 'made' my ecumenical career, Wim without whom I
would never have written the *Dessein de Dieu*"). All these recollections
were accompanied by a "looking forward, with immense curiosity", to
eternity. "Being finite we cannot know what eternity is, we can only
believe it — because Jesus Christ has risen. A belief which at certain
times is absent, or weak. It is difficult to believe without seeing, without
experiencing that Presence which sometimes overflows me with peace
and joy." Such a prayerful remembering of the past and anticipation of the
future filled the silence of the bare hospital room, and in fact it is one of
the secrets of living as one grows older.

Suzanne was equally interested in the present. She read books about
what was happening in America, observed life in the hospital and made
friends with the nurses. This interest in the here-and-now was another
way of coping with old age. It is astonishing how open and curious she
remained about the experiences of young people, whatever their religious
or political convictions. One of her many godchildren, Karin Rodhe,
recalls how as a radical student she visited Suzanne in the Paris of 1968.
Her Marxist books had been confiscated at the airport; that worried
Suzanne who was concerned about the way the French police treated
foreigners. Karin was impressed by her godmother's "intense involvement", "quick perception of significant events and concern for people less

privileged", and the way she could share and talk about the concerns of a radical student of the sixties.

Another godchild, Christoph Baker, often saw "aunt Suzanne" in Paris, on vacations in Switzerland and during Suzanne's last years of life in Strasbourg. Not theology but political interests, and above all playing scrabble simultaneously in English and French, brought them together. A last game, which Christoph Baker lost, was played in 1980. He described their fellowship as "'Zen and the art of scrabble-playing', for the games were a kind of setting of the stage for long conversations about questions of life. Aunt Suzanne was very concerned about my intellectual and political development." In the years immediately after 1968 Suzanne encouraged him to question many things. They spoke about international affairs or French politics, about involvement, injustices in the world and the trap of ideologies. "During these conversations she was never condescending or moralizing or, what would have been worse, pedantic. I always felt I was with a friend of my own age who had simply lived much, much more than I had." Christoph wondered about his deep friendship with a person sixty years older than himself. Was it due to Suzanne's infirmity and the assistance she needed? "I prefer to think", he concluded, "that in fact it was because aunt Suzanne knew how to remain young until the end of her life."

Yet the body, and sometimes also the mind, grew old. "Suddenly I felt as if I was saturated with the Bible and for some time I dropped everything," Suzanne wrote in 1969 after the great labour of rewriting the *Renouveau biblique*, yet the same letter says that "after weeks of laziness" she again took up serious exegetical reading. Two years earlier she had confessed that for the first time in her life she was afraid to travel. Yet physical weariness did not prevent her from visiting Sweden in 1977, and from flying to Rome only a few weeks before her death. However, writing, and then reading too, became difficult. At the end Suzanne must have understood what Preiss told her in 1950, shortly before his death. He still had many plans for writing and teaching and that last letter was full of them, but he also wrote: "I have discovered a strange joy in knowing that, just like everybody else, I am a useless servant. It is a marvellous thing to know that God does not need us, and that, when we become silent, the stones will cry out. This certainty gives such a freedom."

The cross

At the centre of Suzanne's whole life and work stood the cross of Christ. Her very first extant Bible study outline (1911) dealt with the passion story in Mark's gospel. In her first published essay (1912) she presented Jesus' death on the cross as the manifestation and accomplishment of the "divine law of sacrifice", the "divine law of solidarity and love" which alone can give salvation, and meaning to human life and history. Her three meditations on the cross at the 1936 passion week retreat in Uruguay have become a classic. The cross was at the heart of her ecumenical commitment: "Ecumenism must be lived and suffered. We face impossibilities. And it is through these very impossibilities that we are led anew to the cross of Christ, to this certainty of his victory which we all share."[1] The exposition of the cross and meditation on its significance run right through Suzanne's whole work. "The cross of Golgotha is like a stupendous hand-to-hand fight where God takes upon himself the whole burden of all our betrayals and abdications, suffering their consequences and triumphing over them," she wrote during that critical first month of the second world war.[2]

We might expect that this continuous reflection on the cross would be directly related to her own sufferings and infirmity. This is seldom the case. Suzanne coped with her physical handicap with anger and humour, not complaints or theological rationalizations. When she makes a link between her sufferings and the cross it always points away from herself to Christ. In 1922, after years of physical and spiritual suffering, she wrote in her journal: "I consider these physical weaknesses as a grace of God. They force me to stop when the whirlpool of activities could mean less than obedience. The year 1921 was the year of grace when I was ill. God enabled me to fix my eyes on the cross. The cross is a mystery which saves those who contemplate it. Theological explanations only tend to obscure it."

When many years later she lay in the hospital room in the USA, she wrote about her bodily suffering in a lighter vein, referring to her body as "Brother Ass": "When I try to use the big stick on Brother Ass for getting him to advance, he lies down and pretends to be exhausted. And we lose time instead of gaining it. Lord, how little grip the spirit has on the body. Yet let us not be ungrateful: I have used this limping donkey for travelling everywhere. Will this accident be the end of all the journeys?"

Christ's cross and human sufferings are related, but for Suzanne the pain of others came before her own. "God has treated me with leniency. He did not give me the 'grace of suffering for him' as Saint Paul said." She made her own the words of Suzanne Bidgrain who, for eleven years of active ministry, had 34 years of illness, twenty of them years of continual suffering. But she accepted it with grace. "Why should I revolt at my own suffering, if I have not revolted at the suffering of others?"[3] Suzanne's last extant meditation on the cross is a short, hand-written Maundy Thursday note of Holy Week 1975. In it she wonders why she has increasing difficulty in celebrating the high seasons of the church's liturgical calendar. Is it a weakening of faith? Or is it rather caused by the awareness that such feast-days tend to become simply an "act of remembrance", often with sentimental overtones, while ongoing present realities are ignored? At the cross God has taken upon himself our whole existence, and invites us to take upon ourselves the struggles of our fellow human beings, their betrayals and their hopes. "Jesus suffered for some hours a horrible death, but many who were crucified knew the same physical agony. The meaning of the cross lies elsewhere: the cross is the sign and guarantee of the crucified love of God for his creation. Yes, 'Jesus is in agony until the end of time'. His love continues to be mocked at, rejected, caricatured by our cowardice and denials. Jesus agonizes with the hundreds of Vietnamese refugees, with all the persecuted on this earth. 'One must not sleep at such a time' (Pascal). The struggle continues. It is the role of the Holy Spirit to keep up this struggle... Why does he not act more strongly? Mystery of God who knocks on the door but does not break it down. Frightening freedom which includes the right to suicide, the physical but also the spiritual one."[4]

The cross was the centre but not the last word in Suzanne's life. She had learned from the evangelists, especially from John, that the cross as the crucified love of God is paradoxically a victory. The cross and all of human life and history are to be seen in the light of Christ's resurrection. A later piece draws out the lines from the cross to the biblical hope — notes for a message she gave in 1977, based on the Book of Revelation. Suzanne points to the strange paradox that in biblical faith it is a slaughtered lamb that holds the key to the meaning and end of history: a most unpopular image in times of loud economic claims and crude power politics. There is an omnipotence of love that is affirmed in a consciously offered impotence of obedience. To live under the sign of the Lamb is to discern the signs of the times, unmasking the rebellious powers. It also means to believe in Christ's victory at the very hour when, to all appearances, this victory is denied. Faith "lets us become participants of Christ's resurrection, and in the very depth of our being carriers of an invincible hope, a hope which embraces the whole of humanity".[5]

The fourth dimension

"It is the future of the church and the world which interests me."
When Suzanne said this in 1971 she was not thinking merely of the 1980s
or the third millennium. Beyond the three-dimensional earthly reality in
which we live, in hope she could look towards a new heaven and a new
earth. In 1970 three of her close friends had died, Marc Boegner, Paul
Evdokimov and André Philip. Earlier other friends had passed beyond our
space and time. The veil between the realities of this world and the reality
of eternity was becoming thinner. However, Suzanne grew old at a time
and in an environment that had lost much of the sensitivity for transcend-
ence. Hendrik Kraemer had written to her about the inevitable increase of
"a religious atrophy as a result of growing secularism". Orthodox icons
are painted two-dimensionally, for the iconographers say that the third
dimension must be that of eternity which breaks into our human realities.
Suzanne expressed a similar truth in a different way. She was too much of
a scientific observer to ignore the earthly third dimension, but she also
saw that human life can become imprisoned in these earthly space limits.
Therefore she began to speak about a fourth dimension, and wrote in 1965
to D.T. Niles: "My feeling is that our Western civilization is losing the
sense of what I call the fourth dimension — the spiritual dimension of
life." God and prayer then become unreal concepts.

Suzanne had much empathy with her contemporaries who suffered
from this religious atrophy and loss of the fourth dimension. Was her own
faith affected by it? Or was it out of sympathy for those who questioned
Christian faith that she herself began to question many things? It is
impossible to answer this because there are no intimate journals of that
time and Suzanne was always very discreet about discussing her own
problems. However, the correspondence with her Finnish friend Aarne
Siirala in 1971-72 shows that around her eightieth birthday she passed
through a difficult period in her journey of faith. Aarne had visited her
and shared with her his doubts and uncertainties. He felt that many
Christians and churches failed in their task. Suzanne had shared with him
her own experience. Following up that conversation she wrote a letter to
Aarne clarifying what she had said to him about her "doubts and
problems". That letter became what she herself called in the final
paragraph "a queer confession of faith" and it is worth quoting at length.

"It is true that I have gone these last years through a kind of tunnel. I
have felt the impact of the tremendous wave of uncertainty which shakes
our whole world, Christians and theologians included. Maybe my faith
and my prayer life were not strong enough to resist the shock. More

questions were raised in my mind than in the sixty preceding years of my life.

"I am slowly getting out of the tunnel. Intellectually doubt is always possible. In hours of depression the certainties on which we have staked our life may seem questionable. At such moments we lose touch with the deepest realities of life and we have to struggle to recover them.

"I cannot doubt the guidance of God on my life, nor on the life of so many friends whose faith has been a victorious one to the end. Nor can I doubt that God, in a mysterious and hidden way, works in and through history. But I take seriously the freedom of man which can cooperate with or counteract the free self-giving of God. Jesus Christ is for me 'truth lived', God's justice and love incarnate in a human existence: my trust in him, my love for him remain the basic reality of my life. I believe in his victory over sin and death; in his *possible* victory over all the demonic forces of our present world.

"I told you my difficulty in believing in my own survival; it is a question which does not bother me. I leave it to God to do with me what He pleases. I simply do not understand what a general resurrection may mean; it is beyond my human understanding; which does not mean that it cannot exist. I have lost several close friends in the last two years. I am sure their work has not been in vain and their life goes on bearing fruit 'in Christ' in some mysterious way.

"I share with my time a primary concern for the destiny of this world, its search for justice, its hope. I hunger and thirst for the coming of the kingdom, whatever form it takes. I see very destructive forces at work; but also positive signs of renewal. I also know that the 'new world' can only be God's creation.

"My approach to the Bible has been enriched rather than handicapped by recent exegetical research. But if my books with all their limitations have helped some people to see God at work in history and drawn a few closer to Christ, this is enough to be thankful for."[6]

It is difficult to know what the many questions raised in Suzanne's mind were. Two of them appear already in the "Reflections of an Old Woman". There she talks about an autobiography which she had just read of Dorothy Day, an American who grew up in an anarchist milieu and became a Catholic and a militant champion of the poor, living according to the spirit of the sermon on the mount. Twice the words of the Italian/German Catholic thinker Romano Guardini are quoted: "The church is the cross on which Christ is nailed; one cannot separate the Christ from his cross." For Suzanne it was "a terrible word". Terrible not because she thought it was not true. She had written much about the church. Her last essay on this subject was written in 1960, and dealt with the much-debated theme "Mary, Figure of the Church" in an ecumenically sensitive way. She loved the church and helped others to love it, but increasingly the churches' disunity, their lack of courage and faith, became a heavy burden for her. The church was indeed Christ's cross.

Suzanne was increasingly preoccupied with yet another question. In her "Reflections" she wrote: "The Episcopal Church in the USA prays for those who 'died in faith'. Unavoidably I think *of the others.*" The destiny of those who did not know Christ or who rejected him was much on Suzanne's mind. The tension grew between her strong Christocentric belief and the all-embracing, cosmic hope which animated her whole life. Is Christ the only way? What is the truth hidden in the many religious and secular faiths? She did not ask these questions explicitly, but they must have troubled her. In a letter of 1970 to Gibson Winter, a former member of the Parishfield community, Suzanne referred to an article by the French Orthodox thinker Olivier Clément on "Purification by Atheism" and added: "I would despair if I did not still believe that God is at work in history in some mysterious way, allowing old structures to be destroyed in order that new forces might break through... The very fact that so many Christian values are put in question may open the way for a far-reaching renewal."

Praise

Suzanne had more than the biblical span of seventy or eighty years (Ps. 90:10). In her apartment in Paris she still led a weekly Bible study group. Every summer she spent in a chalet near the Mont Blanc range, contemplating the majesty of the mountains and receiving friends. Then the time came when it was impossible for her to go on living alone in her Paris flat, despite the assistance of Rose, her faithful maid, and of volunteer helpers, and despite the company of nephews and CIMADE workers. In February 1978 Marion and Ken Baker, who then worked in Strasbourg, organized Suzanne's move to Emmaus, a retirement home kept by the deaconesses of Strasbourg. This brought her close to the much-loved forests of Alsace, but the deaconess environment was a little too pious for her, and she did not like the fact that they spoke Alsatian most of the time. While she loved the city of Strasbourg it was not her Paris. Many friends visited her in her "exile". The Baker family invited her to their home almost every week-end, but then to Suzanne's great distress they had to move to Rome in 1980 on a new assignment. André

Appel, the president of the Lutheran Church in Alsace, together with his wife Marjory, took over the role the Bakers had played. Friends from CIMADE and the Equipes de recherche biblique came from Paris to see her, among them Irène Poznansky, a former CIMADE team member from Dakar, and Sylviane Moussat who had been a self-effacing friend for over fifty years. During the last few years Suzanne's dear nephew, Bicky Trew from Vancouver Island, had come over to spend summer vacations with his aunt.

Suzanne knew that her life was coming to its end. She often played a game of scrabble all by herself. Increasingly she lived on the border between this world and eternity. Franck Forget, an old friend who visited her often during these last years, wrote: "She knew how to obliterate the frontiers between time and eternity." In what may be the last extant letter hand-written by Suzanne she wrote: "The silence and the solitude in which I now live for the most part make meditation easier. It also develops a sense of the presence of God which accompanies us days and nights. This means that I never feel I am alone, and I am happy here. Humanly speaking I am privileged; a nice room with my own furniture, a bay window with a view on beautiful trees. I watch out for the coming of spring."

Suzanne still had one great wish: she wanted to go and visit the Bakers in Rome. The deaconesses and her friends were worried. Now almost ninety and seriously handicapped, could she make it? Which airline would accept her as a passenger? But Suzanne was keen to do it, and she found friends to organize the journey. In early November 1980 she was carried onto the plane in Strasbourg and settled in an aisle seat. Friends asked her: "Are you happy now?" The response was typical: "No! I want a window seat so I can see the Alps!"

The visit was a great success. In December Suzanne came back to Strasbourg full of the sights which she had seen: the range of the Mont Blanc and the scenes and sights of Rome. Towards the end of her "Roman holiday" she said: "Now I am going back and I want to die."

By early January 1981 it was clear that Suzanne was going. Bicky Trew flew in from Vancouver and stayed with her during the last days. He was in a dilemma. He was convinced that the life of his aunt should not be prolonged as she was no longer able to function normally and he knew that Suzanne would have liked to be helped to die. Yet as one who had no links with the churches he did not want to shock some of her Christian friends who might have been appalled by such a suggestion. He later confided to someone he fully trusted: "I believe they were mistaken with regard to the religious level of my aunt; she was very pragmatic." Others besides Suzanne's nephew, especially the Appels and Moussat, accompanied Suzanne through the last difficult hours. The latter wrote later about the last words Suzanne said to her: "When you hear of my death, just say 'Hallelujah'."

Suzanne died on 24 January 1981, at the end of the Week of Prayer for Christian Unity. On the day which would have been her ninetieth birthday she was buried in a beautiful valley in the northern Vosges, at Windstein near Niederbronn. Several barons and baronesses de Dietrich are also buried in the cemetery of Windstein, but Suzanne's grave is not among the impressive rows of aristocratic tombs. It is among those of common people, a simple flat stone with the symbol of the cross and the inscription:

"Mon âme, bénis l'Eternel!"

"Praise the Lord, my soul!"

NOTES

[1] SdD, "Expériences œcuméniques", *Foi et vie*, 1960, p.183.
[2] SdD, "Parole de l'Eternel", *Le semeur*, November 1939, p.10.
[3] SdD, "Suzanne Bidgrain", *The Student World*, 1962, p.90.
[4] SdD, manuscript note on *Semaine sainte 1975*.
[5] SdD, typed notes on *Sous le signe de l'Agneau*, 1977.
[6] SdD, letter of 29 November 1971 to Aarne Siirala.

Acknowledgments

Much of the work of ordering and cataloguing the letters, manuscripts and documents of the Suzanne de Diétrich Papers (the Fonds Suzanne de Diétrich) was done by Thérèse Klipffel. First of all, I should like to thank her and the staff of the Alsatian section of the National and University Library in Strasbourg, who allowed me full access to these Papers. I would also like to thank the World Student Christian Federation and the library of the World Council of Churches for helping me find relevant material in their archives.

During the three years I spent researching and writing this book, my wife Ineke and I had the joy of getting to know some of the beautiful places that were dear to Suzanne, especially the region around Niederbronn in northern Alsace, and the Algonquin Park and Vancouver Island in Canada. The project also gave us the opportunity to renew old friendships and make new friends. However, it was a time-consuming enterprise, and for many tasks at home, in the garden, and related to the family Ineke was not able to depend on her husband. I am deeply grateful to her for putting up so graciously with my relapse into this exacting work during our retirement.

Special thanks go to Simone Frutiger and Violaine de Montmollin who both read the various drafts and made helpful suggestions for rewriting, as well as to T.K. Thomas and the staff of the publications department of the World Council of Churches for editing the manuscript and seeing it through the press.

In Europe and North America I recorded interviews about Suzanne de Diétrich with the following persons who knew her at different periods of her life and in various work relationships: Malou Achard, Soeur Albertine, Andry Andrews, André Appel, Marjory Appel, Marion Baker, Madeleine Barot, Emma-Lou Benignus, A. de Blonay, Erica Brucker, Inga-Brita Castren, Marie-Jeanne Coleman-de Haller, André Dumas, Ilse Friedeberg, Soeur Irène, Simone Mathil, Jacques Maury, Roger Mehl, Sylvaine Moussat, Elisabeth Palmer, Irène Poznanski, Catherine

Schneider, Théo Schneider, Renée Sturm, Michael Trew and Helen Turnbull. Many of them also provided letters and photographs. Written recollections and information material were provided by Dora Atger, Christoph Baker, Elisabeth Behr-Sigel, André Blanchet, Violette Blanchet, Edouard Blancy, Suzanne Conord, Jeanne Couve, Frank G. Engel, D. Dorian, Lucie l'Epplatenier, John Garrett, Hélène Georger-Vogt, Francis House, Charles Johnston, Berthie Lasserre, Betty Layton, Alice Leenhardt, Jacqueline Leuba, Steven Mackie, Robert Martin-Achard, Etienne Mathiot, Hans Mayr, Henry Mellon, Glenda Pawsey, Colette Preiss, William Perkins, Cheryl Pontier-Rogers, Birgit Rodhe, Karin Rodhe, André Roux, Elisabeth Schmidt, Michael Trew, Mukuna Tshitebua, Henri Vernier, Marie Vincent, Gibson Winter and Sara Winter.

All this was an invaluable help in understanding the background of many details in Suzanne de Diétrich's life, correspondence and work. The written material has been incorporated into the Papers in Strasbourg.